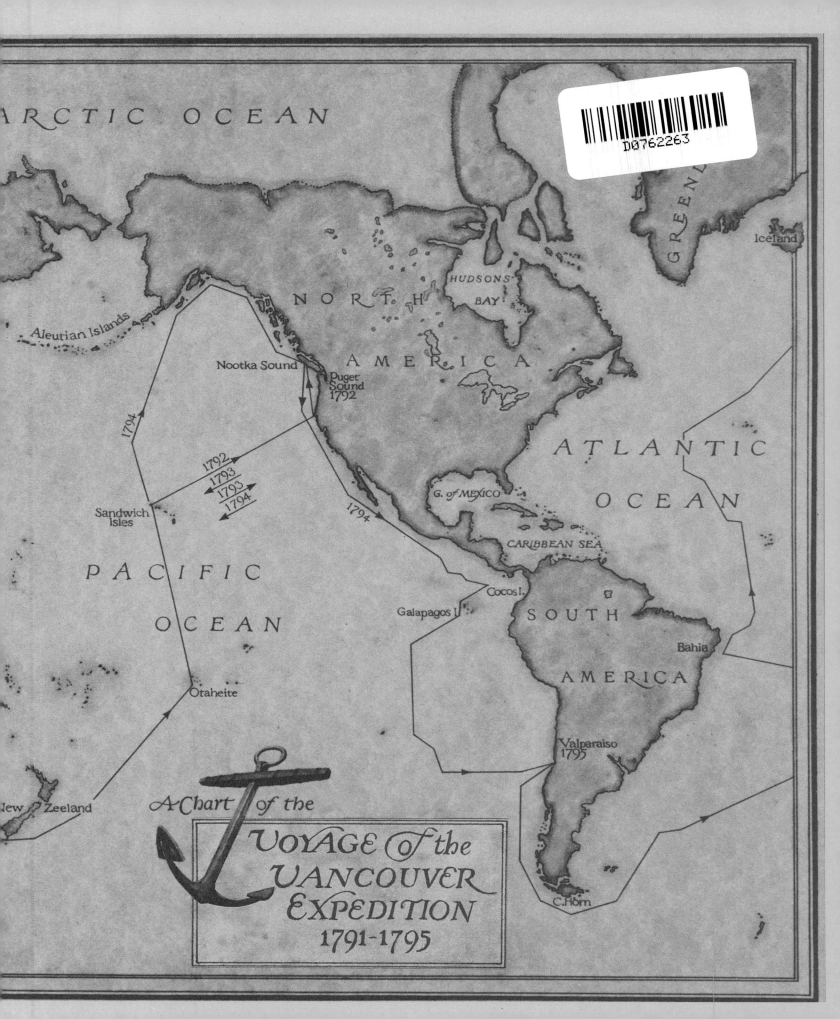

ARCTIC OCEAN

GREENLAND

Iceland

Aleutian Islands

NORTH AMERICA

HUDSONS BAY

Nootka Sound

Puget Sound 1792

1794

ATLANTIC OCEAN

1792
1793
1793
1794

Sandwich Isles

1794

G. of MEXICO

PACIFIC OCEAN

CARIBBEAN SEA

Cocos I.

Galapagos I.

SOUTH AMERICA

Bahia

Otaheite

Valparaiso 1795

New Zeeland

C. Horn

A Chart of the

VOYAGE of the VANCOUVER EXPEDITION 1791-1795

D0762263

4700

Lieutenant on the Vancouver Expedition,
British naval officer for whom Mt. Baker was named

JOSEPH BAKER

By Robert C. Wing

Gray Beard Publishing
Seattle, Washington

Printed and bound in Hong Kong

First published in an edition of 2,500.

©1992 Robert C. Wing

All rights reserved. No part of this book may be reproduced or transmitted in any form or by any means, electronic or mechanical, including photocopying, recording or information storage and retrieval systems now known or to be invented, without permission in writing from the publisher, except that brief passages may be quoted for reviews.

Library of Congress Cataloging in Publication Data

Wing, Robert C.   1921-
  Joseph Baker: Lieutenant on the Vancouver Expedition,
British naval officer for whom Mt. Baker was named.

  Bibliography.
  Includes index.
  1. Puget Sound area—Discovery and exploration.
2. Northwest Coast of North America—Discovery and
exploration. 3. Baker, Joseph. 4. Explorers—Washington
State—Biography.
92-73372

ISBN 0-933686-02-1

Published by Gray Beard Publishing
              1735 Westlake Ave. N., Suite 207
              Seattle, WA 98109
              (206) 285-3171

Book and cover design: Ben Dennis
Cover photo: Lee Mann
Cover painting: Steve Mayo
Production: Cheryl Butler, Paul Kotz, Jeanie Baldwin, all of Ben
    Dennis and Associates, Seattle, Washington
Maps created for this book: rendering by Ray Braun
Typestyle: Palatino
Printed and bound in Hong Kong

PREFACE

My interest in Joseph Baker first developed as a by-product of the research for the biography of Peter Puget, published in 1979. Puget was the British naval officer for whom beautiful Puget Sound in western Washington State was named. Baker, a fellow naval officer on the Vancouver expedition, was similarly honored with the designation of Mt. Baker as the name of the prominent peak located inland from the northern reaches of Puget Sound.

The story of Mt. Baker, the mountain, has been amply told by others—its geology, early climbers, its place in the lore of the regional Native Americans. This is the first-told story of Joseph Baker, the man—a story of 18th century action adventure which could have been fashioned by C.S. Forester as another of his Horatio Hornblower naval hero series. I say it "could have been," but it wasn't! For this is the factual account of the training, the trials, the triumphs, and the personal tragedies from which were formed the kind of naval leaders able, in the late 18th century, to open the way to new parts of a still partially unknown world.

Joseph Baker never set foot on Mt. Baker. But now, 200 years after he was here on Puget Sound, some of his descendants have come to visit and to settle within view of that mountain. They bring with them the same wonder and curiosity which must have motivated Joseph Baker and his fellow shipmates to spend over four years of their lives helping to chart the way—the way to a region and a way of life so many of us are privileged to enjoy.

ROBERT C. WING
Lakebay, Washington, U.S.A.

3

JUN 2 0 1994

FOREWORD

Elizabeth Baker, circa 1802.

Richard Baker, Inverness, Scotland.

Joseph Baker at the rank of Captain, circa 1802.

Richard Baker, Inverness, Scotland.

I remember well the time I first flew into Vancouver in the September of 1982, descending from 33,000 feet and observing Mt. Baker's peak "towering above the clouds"—to use the words of Capt. Vancouver, but from an angle that he could hardly have imagined! Ever since then the mountain has been a special place for me, and something of the air of pilgrimage surrounds a family trip to it.

The mystique of living within range of Mt. Baker has been reinforced for me by the experience of climbing the rigging of a tall ship in the Juan de Fuca Strait—with its accompanying sense of historical *deja vu*—and by the further experience of rowing in a replica of one of Capt. Vancouver's ship's boats which are now being handcrafted locally for the bicentenary of the 1792 event.

That is not to say that the family connection can tell the whole story. Regardless of the name which history has delivered to it, Mount Baker has an intrinsic majesty and beauty, which is captivating whether one is hiking along its trails at 6000 feet, or simply looking out of an office window at its crisp silhouette, a hundred miles distant, against a purple and orange sky.

Of course, two hundred years is not long in the history of a mountain. The current name of "Mt. Baker" must be placed not only in the context of geological time, but also in human perspective, with full respect to all those before and since Vancouver's expedition who have looked upon the mountain with awe, fear, or faith, and have given it a name. Nevertheless, in terms of seafaring and scientific exploration, these two full centuries have told us a long story of human achievement. And in this I can feel a solidarity which spans the generations and a gratitude for what I know of the life of Capt. Joseph Baker.

As I look back at the more recent events of 1991, I consider myself privileged, in my work here at Malaspina College in Nanaimo, to have taken part in the Spanish celebrations of the original Malaspina voyage which crossed paths, under Galiano and Valdes, with the *Discovery* and the *Chatham*. And at the time of writing, I am looking forward to the re-enactment of the British exploration and the re-telling of the lives of people whose names, like Baker's, have come to dominate our local landscape.

Robert Wing's engaging biography of Joseph Baker sets before us a man who fastidiously recorded and charted for posterity what had never been put on paper before; a man of worldwide exploration, yet a family man of small towns and rural roots; a man of patience and precision, yet a man of action and enterprise; a man of faith and a man of science; a man who left as a legacy an example of disciplined leadership combined with a spirit of adventure.

The reading of this book stirs in me an awareness that I belong to the past and the future every bit as much as I belong to the living present. And my view of the rare winter sun rising over Mt. Baker on a clear morning stirs in me a further wish—a hope that my children can cultivate and pass on in their generation an appreciation of their ancestor's contribution, not only in the names that they bear, but in an exploration of the qualities recorded of Joseph Baker in this account.

ANDREW D. TWIDDY, M.A.,
Great,Great,Great
Grandson of Joseph Baker
Nanaimo, B.C.

TABLE OF CONTENTS

* Whenever material has been quoted from an outside source, such as an expedition journal, the grammar and spelling of the original have been preserved.

CHAPTER 1

Mt. Baker—Ho!

Joseph Baker, age twenty-four, a veteran of nearly eleven years of Royal Navy service, now third lieutenant of His Majesty's sloop-of-war *Discovery*, surveyed the scene from the quarter deck on this misty April morning. He was carefully checking the log board, the wind, the sea, and the crew as he prepared to assume the morning watch at 4:00 a.m.

The *Discovery* rode at anchor in the Pacific Ocean about three miles south of Destruction Island and three miles off the northwest coast of the land later to become part of the State of Washington, U.S.A. The ship's log showed the day to be April 29, 1792.

Lt. Baker was well aware of the origin of the name, Destruction Island—the 1775 visit of Spanish explorer, Bodega y Quadra, during which a boat crew, attempting to replenish their fresh water supply at the mouth of the adjacent Hoh River, was ambushed and murdered by Native Americans.[1] A nearly identical experience had befallen a boat crew from the American trading ship, *Imperial Eagle*, Capt. C.W. Barkley in 1787.

This morning Lt. Baker had little time to spend reminiscing history. He was well aware that his commanding officer, Captain George Vancouver, always a stern master, often petulant, would be impatient for progress northward along the coast. All felt certain that the entrance to the Straits of Juan de Fuca which they were seeking was but a few miles ahead. Weak winds and adverse currents encountered the past two days had nourished the Captain's frustration at not having achieved that immediate goal.

Lt. Baker had been up and about well in advance of the 4:00 a.m. start of his assigned morning watch. Finding light breezes from a favorable quarter, he made the signal to the consort armed tender, *H.M.S. Chatham* to weigh anchor. He likewise ordered the *Discovery* crew to weigh anchor and "come-to-sail under single reefed topsails and topgallant sails......". The lookout struck eight bells signalling the end of the midwatch and the start of Baker's morning watch. On April 29, sunrise at this latitude was yet an hour away. As Baker peered through the twilight to assess the general situation, the lookout sounded out, "...strange sail to the southwest!".

Destruction Island, off Washington State coast.

Vancouver's ships Discovery *and* Chatham *rendezvous with Gray's ship* Columbia *near Destruction Island. Puget and Menzies in longboat approach* Columbia *for parley.*
Parker McCallister-Artist, Seattle Times Newspaper, and Seattle Public Library.

Capt. Vancouver was summoned on deck immediately! From his journal we get the following account of the ensuing events:

"At four o'clock, a sail was discovered to the westward standing in (toward) shore. This was a great novelty, not having seen any vessel but our own consort during the last eight months. She soon hoisted American colours, and fired a gun to leeward. At six we spoke her. She proved to be the ship *Columbia*, commanded by Mr. Robert Gray, belonging to Boston, whence she had been absent nineteen months. Having little doubt of his being the same person who had formerly commanded the sloop *Washington*, I desired he would bring to, and sent Mr. Puget and Mr. Menzies on board to acquire such information as might be serviceable in our future operations."

Menzies' journal provides a colorful account of the discussion with Gray, in part as follows:

"...I accompanied Lt. Puget in order to obtain what information we could, & the reader may easily conceive the eagerness with which we interrogated the Commander when we found.....that here at the entrance of Juan de Fuca's Streights we should meet the very man (who) in his former voyage had gone up (those) streights in the sloop *Washington* about 17 leagues[2] in an East by South direction & finding he did not meet with encouragement as a trader to pursue it further, he returned back & came out to sea again."

Gray regaled them with lurid tales of intrigues and murder his crew had suffered at the hands of the Natives. The accounts were based in fact, but presented in a manner to discourage any would-be fur trading competitors.

When Puget and Menzies returned to the *Discovery* with word that the entrance they sought to Juan de Fuca's Straits was only a few miles further north, full sail was promptly resumed.

This most fortunate encounter between Gray's ship *Columbia* and Vancouver's *Discovery* and *Chatham* was duly noted in the logs of both parties. Apparently neither of these proud captains wished to defer to the other by requesting permission for a personal visit. Thus the historical record was denied witness to an encounter between two very strong, very different personalities, each engaged in parallel activities, the results of which would play a powerful role in the subsequent resolution of international land claims and boundary determinations. As more completely documented in other biographical references, Gray was a Yankee fur trader, fiercely driven by entrepreneurial objectives. But he was also possessed of great curiosity which frequently lead him to take foolhardy risks in the face of an interesting challenge. Thus it was he who, just two weeks later, discovered the mighty river he named Columbia, the entrance to which had eluded, or frightened off, numerous earlier explorers.[3] Vancouver on the other hand, was a "by-the-book" naval officer, at times a brutal disciplinarian, totally dedicated to accomplishing the several goals spelled out in his mission orders.

Another interesting note of comparison is offered by the personal logs of two junior officers, John Boit, junior mate aboard the *Columbia*, and Joseph Baker, 3rd Lieutenant on the *Discovery*. Boit, 17 years of age was a bright young lad out of Boston with over two years of experience at sea, and with demonstrated abilities in writing and navigation. He kept the only complete log of Gray's second world circumnavigation voyage.[4] Baker, 24, was an equally accomplished young officer, born in Bristol, England, already with nearly eleven years of naval service and with proven skills in navigation and especially chartmaking. Both of these promising young men would later rise to assignments as ship captains.

On this day, however, an interesting difference in their personal logs is worthy of explanation. Boit recorded the date as April 28, 1792, whereas Baker's log shows it to be April 29, 1792. Some have questioned the accuracy of at least one of these records. After all, are we to believe that either of these navigators, able to find their way around the world using the changing positions of the sun, moon, and stars, didn't know what day it was? No, in fact both logs are correct within the conventions of that era. The explanation is most easily grasped if we picture retracing Vancouver's path, not in 1792, but in say 1992. Vancouver traveled an easterly path from England to Australia to North America. If we followed that path today, somewhere midway between Australia and North America we would cross the International Date Line, and repeat one day on the calendar. No such convention was recognized in 1792. At that time ships circumnavigating the globe kept the calendar based on the point of departure. They routinely made the adjustment (skipping a day if sailing east to west and repeating a day if west to east) at or near the end of the voyage. It was not until 1884 that United States President Chester Arthur convened the conference of world representatives that adopted the convention of the International Date Line, to be located in mid-Pacific Ocean (generally longitude 180°) as the meridian at which all navigators would make the necessary adjustment. Had that convention been established in 1792, Vancouver's crew would have repeated a day enroute to the Sandwich Islands (Hawaii), and Baker's log would have agreed with Boit's.

The *Discovery* and *Chatham* moved north, holding within 2 or 3 miles of shore. About noon they reached the south shore of the entrance to the Juan de Fuca Straits. Vancouver ordered *Discovery* to reduce sail, and signalled *Chatham* to take the lead in entering between the north shore of Tatoosh Island and a large rock lying further to the north. Cruising at a leisurely pace along the southerly shore of the Strait, the ships immediately attracted the attention of the local natives, the residents of the present day village of Neah Bay. Waving off the polite offers of the natives to come aboard for trade, the ships anchored about 12 miles inside the Straits. The wily Captain Gray had followed them into the Straits, apparently to verify whether they were, in fact, on a charting mission, or were another fur trading competitor to worry about. He must have seen something to calm his concerns, for he shortly returned to his own trading route on the coastal shores.

The next morning, April 30, 1792 (by Vancouver's calendar), the little squadron proceeded on into the Straits following an easterly course along the coast of what is now known as the Olympic Peninsula. They were favored with "a gentle breeze...from the northwest attended with clear and pleasant weather...," which certainly facilitated the continuing business of surveying and charting the shoreline. The look-out at the foremast top was ordered to study the shore ahead in search for a sheltered harbor where the ships might be safely anchored to attend the many maintenance requirements which had accumulated after months at sea. Vancouver swept the landscapes to the north, east and south, with his glass, assessing the character of the area. And Baker was also studying the surroundings, and making the rough sketches which would later be the basis of detailed charts.

Vancouver noted that at "about five in the afternoon, a long, low, sandy point of land was observed projecting from the cliffy shores into the sea, behind which was seen the appearance of a well-sheltered bay, and a little to the southeast of it, an opening in the land, promising a safe and extensive port...which from its great resemblance to Dungeness in the British channel I called New Dungeness....". Vancouver also noted, "About this time a very high conspicuous craggy mountain, bearing by compass N. 50° E. (was) discovered by the third Lieutenant, and in compliment to him called by me *Mount Baker*." Vancouver also described Mt. Baker as towering above the clouds, covered with snow, and at a very remote distance.

Seventy years would pass before this splendid mountain would yield its isolation to a party of climbers, and that party was to be lead by another Englishman. Edmund T. Coleman, born in England in 1824, was trained as a librarian, a botanist, and was an accomplished artist. His real passion, however, was mountain climbing. He became a charter member of the Alpine Club of London, qualifying with extensive experience in the Swiss Alps. Wearying of the throngs he encountered on the well traversed slopes of Europe, Coleman determined to explore the unexplored peaks of the North American west.

His first step was to move to Victoria, Vancouver Island in 1862. From there Mt. Baker

Mt. Baker aglow in the afternoon sun. Occasional steam venting from the south face evidences continuing thermal activity beneath the mountain. Mt. Baker is located approximately 30 miles east of Bellingham, Washington.

Lee Mann-photographer, Sedro-Woolley.

dominated the eastern horizon on a clear day, and promptly became the focus of Edmund Coleman's attention. Getting established in his newly adopted city took more time than he probably wished, because not until 1866 was he able to launch his first attempt to climb the mountain, and this ended in frustration. Undaunted, he returned in 1868 with a new team of three experienced climbing companions and armed with the knowledge gained from his first attempt. Success was his; he reached the summit on August 17, 1868.

Throughout his preparation and execution of the climbs, Coleman had the assistance of a number of Native Americans who were familiar with the hunting trails on the lower slopes. However, they declined to venture above the snow line, believing that the upper reaches of the mountain were the province of "powerful spirits." The aura of the mountain was described in stories and myths handed down through generations, many laced with colorful explanations of the fearsome volcanos known to have occurred on several occasions in geologic time. Coleman learned that the several tribes living in the vicinity of Mt. Baker had different names for the peak. The most common was understood by the white man to be Koma Kulshan.[5]

In 1790, two years before the arrival of Vancouver, the Spanish explorer, Manuel Quimper, had seen the same mountain and named it "La Gran Montana del Carmelo." However, this fact, like the main body of all Spanish exploration findings, was treated as military intelligence, and not made known to the general public for many decades.

Edmund Coleman reckoned the height of his climbs by carrying a barometer, the accepted technique of the time. On that basis he noted the top of Mt. Baker to be 11,400 feet above sea level. More precise methods applied in later years resulted in fixing the official height at 10,778 feet above sea level. But surely, the mountain never looked higher nor shone brighter than it did to Lieutenant Joseph Baker on that Spring day in 1792, when his alertness and the fortunes of circumstance resulted in his family name being memorialized on that beautiful peak, Mt. Baker.

CHAPTER 2

On-The-Job Training

Joseph Baker was born in the ancient seaport city of Bristol in southwest England, the second son of James and Nancy Baker. The precise date of his birth has been obscured by diverse reports. St. Peter's Church where he was reportedly baptized, usually a reliable type of source in such matters, was destroyed with all its records in the bombing of World War II. Based on the information included on his church memorial stone, prepared under the direction of his widow, he was born in the year of 1768, most likely in February. His mother's maiden name was Ludlow, indicating a probable relationship to the prominent wool industry family of the town of Ludlow, Shropshire, a town which would be the center of important events in Joseph Baker's adult life.

As a "second son," British custom of the time dictated that Joseph could expect to inherit no part of the family business interests or estate. All of the financial assets would go to the oldest son, who would also inherit important responsibilities for the protection of the younger siblings. For younger sons the choice of careers typically narrowed to two, the church ministry or the military. For Joseph Baker the choice was to be an officer in His Majesty's Navy.

The path by which a schoolboy became a King's officer was never an easy one. In mid-eighteenth century there was not yet a naval academy in a university setting, with warm dormitories, well appointed classrooms, sports events on the weekends, and tutoring in the social graces—far from it! The process was entirely on-the-job training of the harshest variety. Each applicant for enlistment as a Midshipman had to demonstrate the ability to read and write, together with skill in basic mathematics. This normally meant completion of grammar school, usually achieved by age twelve or thirteen. Acceptance for naval officer training in eighteenth century England required either influence or money, though a shortage of these "resources" might be overcome through a starting enlistment as cabin boy or an able-bodied (A.B.) seaman.

From the overall record it is apparent that the Baker family lived in comfortable circumstances, but were not to be numbered among the very wealthy. Whether for this reason or simply a matter of available openings, we find Joseph Baker on December 19, 1781, at age thirteen, struggling under the burden of his modestly appointed sea chest, reporting aboard the *H.M.S. Alert*, Captain James Vashon, rated as "Captain's servant."

H.M.S. Alert was a modest size brig-sloop, 78 feet in length with a 25 foot beam, and carrying 14 guns. Typically suited for convoy escort or harbor patrol, she was presently destined for heavier duty. Vashon had recently been promoted to the rank of Commander and ordered home from the Caribbean to his first command, the *Alert*. His orders were to return to the Caribbean and rejoin the large British fleet operating under the command of Admiral Sir George Rodney.

For young Joseph Baker the transition from schoolboy to cabin boy could not have been more abrupt. He was not to be given any time for basic training on harbor patrol, to learn the way of the ship or the ways of his shipmates—to get his sea legs. His introduction to this new career was to take place aboard a 78 foot long sailing vessel, heading out across the north Atlantic Ocean—in December! What could he draw on to help meet this dramatic challenge? It is likely that he had picked up knowledge of ships and ship's lingo around the docks at his home town of Bristol. He must have learned the lessons of discipline and attention to duty from a well ordered school or a strong home. Whatever motivated Joseph, his performance was clearly outstanding. Within two weeks he had been rerated as an able-bodied seaman. By the time they reached the Caribbean, he no doubt had mastered shipboard life, from the meager fare at ship's mess, to the terror ridden task of bending on more sail by scrambling up the ratlines and out along the footlines 100 feet above the rolling deck. In the process he made such a favorable impression on the Captain that Vashon would become his lifelong mentor, in matters that extended far beyond life at sea.

The first port of call in the Caribbean would have been the major British naval base at English Harbor on the south coast of the Island of Antigua.

ATLANTIC OCEAN

NORTH SEA

UNITED KINGDOM

SCOTLAND

Leith

IRELAND

Shannon
Estuary

ENGLAND

Ludlow

Presteigne

London

Bristol

ENGLISH CHANNEL

FRANCE

0   100

Nautical Miles

Often referred to as the Gibraltar of the Caribbean, this port provided anchorage well protected from both tropical hurricanes and marauding French or Spanish fleets. The base was equipped with repair docks, supply warehouses, officer's quarters and administrative offices. At various times it had or would serve as the headquarters of such notable naval heroes as Admiral Sir George Rodney, Admiral Sir Samuel Hood, and the flamboyant Captain (later admiral) Horatio Nelson. By the mid-nineteenth century English Harbor ceased to be able to accommodate the new larger naval ships and the base was abandoned. It has since been restored with all of the original masonry buildings refurbished, and is an important international yachting center.

Whatever English Harbor had been or would be, on that day early in 1782, when *Alert* dropped anchor at the end of an Atlantic crossing, it must have looked like a bit of heaven to Able-Bodied Seaman Joseph Baker. The semi-arid hillsides and the blazing sun of Antigua provided a very welcome change from the stormy north Atlantic. But this was not a vacation cruise. *Alert* needed to be repaired and resupplied, and made ready in every way to carry out her assigned mission in the continuing wars in the Caribbean.

To most Americans the Revolutionary War had ended with the surrender of British General Cornwallis at Yorktown, Virginia, the previous October 19, 1781. The final treaty would not be signed for nearly two years, on September 3, 1783, but the hostilities on American soil essentially ended at Yorktown. In the broader context of world events however, England and France had been at war during most of the previous thirty years, and would be for most of the next thirty. For those two countries the American Revolutionary War was just another important and costly episode, in a continuing struggle to dominate trade routes and colonial empires. The centers of military conflict shifted from the North Sea to the Caribbean to the Mediterranean Sea to the Indian Ocean, and often flared in more than one region at the same time. The end of the focus on the American Colonies had, from a military perspective, simply freed up naval forces, both English and French, to concentrate on the competition to control the then valuable sugar production on the Caribbean Islands.

The formidable British naval forces in the Caribbean area were under the command of Admiral Sir George Rodney, with Admiral Sir Samuel Hood second in command. Separate squadrons operated out of the islands of Jamaica and St. Lucia, in addition to the major base at Antigua. An equally sizeable French fleet operated out of the island of Martinique under the command of crafty Admiral Count Francisco De Grasse. It was De Grasse who positioned the French fleet outside Yorktown in a manner which cut off the British fleet attempting to rescue Cornwallis.

As soon as *Alert* was ready for sea, Captain Vashon received orders to proceed to St. Lucia, about 230

National Maritime Museum, Greenwich, England.

Cabin Boy, sketch by Thomas Rowlandson, circa 1796.

ST. KITTS

NEVIS

ANTIGUA

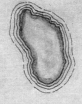 → English Harbour

MONTSERRAT

GUADELOUPE

LES SAINTES

↗ Near here the English fleet under
Admiral Rodney defeated
the French under De Grasse, 1782.

DOMINICA

MARTINIQUE.

CARIBBEAN

SEA

 ST. LUCIA

 ST. VINCENT

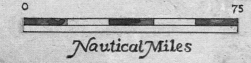

0   75

Nautical Miles

miles to the south, for further assignment. He knew from much experience in the Caribbean that he could count on generally favorable weather and rather steady trade winds, just the conditions he would need to sharpen his ship and crew in battle tactics and maneuvers. Smaller vessels such as the *Alert* were not expected to play an important role in the heavy gunnery of major sea battles—that was the task of the Ships-of-the-Line, the battleships of the day, carrying 70 to 100 cannons arrayed on two or three decks. The *Alert* would be expected to be highly maneuverable, to position herself to relay the critical flag signals up and down the line when the smoke of battle obscured the view between ships. She might be called on to transfer senior officers from a disabled ship to another still in fighting trim, or assist in rescues. Of course she was to be ready to use her light guns whenever called on. Clearly Joseph Baker was getting an accelerated course in naval warfare.

It was late in March 1782, when *Alert* arrived at St. Lucia. The reports of a major land and sea battle on and around the Islands of St. Christopher (St. Kitts) and Nevis were the center of everyone's conversation. Admirals Rodney and Hood were assembling all of the Caribbean squadrons to mount a major attack on De Grasse. During the first week of April, *Alert* was ordered to perform lookout duty off Martinique, keeping an eye on De Grasse. It became apparent that the French fleet was assembling for a major action, and Rodney guessed it would be a move on Jamaica.

Early morning, April 8, the British fleet put to sea from St. Lucia, heading north toward Guadaloupe. Divided into three squadrons, the van (lead) was under the command of Rear Admiral Hood in *HMS Barfleur*. Fleet commander, Admiral Rodney in *HMS Formidable*, was positioned in the center of the second squadron. Bringing up the rear was Rear Admiral Drake in *HMS Princessa* at the head of the third squadron. The entire fleet comprised 36 ships-of-the-line, major battleships carrying from 64 to 90 guns each. In addition there were 19 small faster support vessels, frigates and sloops including *HMS Alert*.

On the morning of April 9, a portion of the French fleet was sighted between the Island of Dominica and the group of small islands just south of Guadaloupe, called the Saintes. The winds had turned a bit fickle, causing center and rear squadrons to fall behind the van. As Hood slowed to let the others catch up, De Grasse's van deftly maneuvered into firing position. There was a brief, indecisive exchange, but De Grasse was not ready to take on the entire British fleet he could see approaching, and so broke off the engagement.

The next two days were occupied in chase and maneuver, with the French able to avoid being put in a disadvantageous position. The textbook maneuver of the time called for Rodney to array his fleet in a single line, parallel to the enemy's similar line, and then draw to within 500 yards (or as close as 50) after which both fleets would fire waves of cannonballs (24 to 32 pounds each) into each others' hulls, decks and masts. For a variation on this theme, the gunners might be ordered to switch to "grape," bucket-sized bundles of lemon-sized iron balls, which shredded sails and mowed deck crews like a scythe. If after a bit of this mayhem an aggressor found one or more of his enemies in a weakened condition, the next step was to send the shipboard marines aloft in the rigging to pepper the enemy's deck with musket fire as the attacking ship drew closer. Finally, if neither ship "struck its colors," and if a few of the cannons below were still firing, barrel-to-barrel, an attempt might be made to board and capture the enemy ship.

Finally on the morning of April 12, in the area just south of the Saintes, Rodney got his fleet into a situation he liked. All of his battleships were in line headed north with Drake's squadron now in the van, Hood's in the rear. De Grasse now had his full fleet, 30 ships-of-the-line, all in line, headed south just a short distance to the east. De Grasse had the weather gage, meaning he was upwind from the British and presumably better able to choose to close-in or to break off the engagement. The scene could well have been orchestrated right out of a text book, but Rodney was not known as a by-the-book Admiral. He was an innovator, willing to try new tactics, even knowing that failure,

Rear Admiral Sir Samuel Hood, who commanded one of the British Naval squadrons at the Battle of the Saintes, 1782.

English Harbor, Antigua, West Indies, now a popular international yachting center.

while not following standard procedures, might bring down the most severe punishment—the firing squad!

Rodney ordered the signal to commence firing. *Marlborough*, the lead ship, opened fire on the center of the French column, and the others followed as the British column moved slowly north, with increasing numbers of their ships coming abreast of the southbound French.

A sudden minor shift in wind at the French van caused a small break in the column—just the sort of break Rodney had prepared for. Following a bold contingency plan, Rodney signalled six of the center squadron ships to follow his flagship, *Formidable*. He turned sharply to the right, passed through the French column, causing a general disarray in the entire French formation. Hood, leading the rear squadron, did not follow Rodney, but rather continued north, thus trapping the French center and rear in fire from both sides. The ensuing melee went on for several hours, amid the thunder of cannon, the crash of masts and rigging, and the smoke and fire of burning ships. The British emerged with one of the major naval victories of the 18th century, but a costly one to both sides. British losses were recorded at 253 killed and 816 wounded, many with amputations. The total of French killed and wounded was reported as 3000. In the language of the time, the "butcher's bill" that day was a heavy one.

Sir Rodney had been a busy man that day, but not too busy to take note of the performance of his captains. He singled out Captain Vashon for special commendation and reward. Vashon had deftly maneuvered *Alert* to relay critical signals, had later taken possession of the French ship *Glorieuse*, and still later had managed to rescue a large number of both British and French seamen following the explosion of the *Caesar*. Vashon's reward, immediate promotion from Commander to the permanent rank of Captain, and reassignment to command of *HMS Prince William*, a ship-of-the-line carrying 64 guns.

The record shows that four days later, on April 16, 1782, another British seaman would be transferred and promoted. Joseph Baker was ordered to report for new duty aboard the *Prince William*, with the rank of Midshipman. As he came aboard the next morning, touching his hat to the quarterdeck, he could well ponder the remarkable changes in his life that had occurred in just five brief months. As recent as the past December, he had been but one of many grammar school graduates, wondering what sort of future lay ahead. Now at age fourteen, he was a veteran of one of the great sea battles of his lifetime, a battle from which Admiral Horatio Nelson would pattern his triumph at Trafalgar in 1805. Though he could not have appreciated that fact at the time, he surely felt the pride of having achieved his first goal—he was officially Midshipman Joseph Baker, officer trainee in the King's Navy.

Baker's assignment to the Prince William was short lived, approximately two months. His mentor, Captain Vashon, was transferred briefly to *HMS Formidable* as flag captain, (that is, captain of a ship on which an admiral maintains his headquarters) and then to command of the frigate, *HMS Sibyl*. Baker was reassigned to follow Vashon in each of these transfers.

By August 1782, the frantic pace of recent months, the battle of the Saintes and the realignment of ship and crew assignments which followed, had passed. Aboard *Sibyl*, the routine quickly settled into the more typical pattern of daily training and drill to gain and maintain the expected skills. For Baker, that routine held special challenges. Midshipmen were afforded a measure of the respect due officers, particularly with respect to the type of punishment meted out for misdeeds, but their accommodations were not better than those of the crew, separate but equally bad. Each Midshipman was required to keep a daily journal noting progress of the ship and any special events, including the administration of all disciplinary actions. These journals were routinely reviewed by a senior officer, and in effect, formed the basis of tutoring in language arts. One of the by-products of this part of the training is the large quantity of well written records and correspondence covering naval history, now available in such archival repositories as the Public Records Office at Kew, a suburb of London. Another part of the daily routine was the study of applied mathematics, usually taught by the Sailing Master, a non-commissioned officer. We often see pictures of mariners standing on a windswept deck taking an observation of the moon or stars using a sextant or octant. What we never see is the laborious process which followed, by which those observations were reduced to a position location on a chart—particularly the tedious process in use in the late 18th century period. By the time a midshipman reached the age of, say sixteen, he would be expected to have greater skills in spherical geometry and trigonometry than would be found from the test scores of most high school graduates in the United States today.

The standard mariner's textbook of the day was *"The New Practical Navigator,"* by John Hamilton Moore.[1] Published in London about every two years starting in

National Maritime Museum, Greenwich, England.
Midshipman, sketch by Thomas Rowlandson, circa 1796.

the 1770s, it comprised approximately five hundred pages covering all aspects of navigation, including tables of trigonometric functions, logarithms, and positions of the sun, moon, Jupiter's moons, and many other astronomical bodies. Also included was basic information on the rigging of a ship, seafaring terminology, and the accepted latitude and longitude of many ports and headlands in the charted portion of the world. According to its subtitle, the book contained, "The Substance of that Examination, every Candidate for a Commission in the Royal Navy and Officer in the Honourable East India Company's Service, must pass through, previous to their being appointed." Demand for the book in America and India reached such high levels as to stimulate a market in forged copies, a problem the author attempted to overcome by including his portrait on the frontpiece of proper originals.

Gun direction and firing practices were included in the training of all midshipmen. Some of this training was conducted aboard ship, but gun crews were often assigned to shore batteries at the entrances to harbors. On occasion they might even be landed to supply artillery support for ground troops.

Another aspect of officer training was the lesson in diligence to duty and risk taking, and the importance of these attributes to individual self-interest. The Admiralty was quick to respond in adjusting the size of the active-duty fleet to the fortunes of war—or peace. When a reduction in forces was called for, a substantial number of ships could be rapidly "laid up in ordinary." Crews were simply paid off. Furloughed officers were put on half-pay. For senior officers, particularly captains and above, the active duty assignments were made on the basis of seniority. But for junior officers, the assignments were arbitrary, influenced by attitude toward duty, willingness to accept dangerous missions, and general reputation among senior officers under whom they had served.

Baker would quickly see how this played out during the reduction in naval forces ordered in late 1783. Vashon, among the most recently appointed captains, was "put on the beach" for two years. Baker was fortunate in being assigned to the *Bombay Castle*, 74 guns, for an uneventful two year tour of duty.

When, in 1786, Vashon was recalled to duty aboard the *Europa*, 50 guns, one of his first acts was to arrange for the reassignment of Joseph Baker to his ship. Midshipman Baker was delighted to report aboard the *Europa* on December 9, 1786. Little could he know the influence on his future career by the acquaintances he would make in this new assignment. His new shipmates included a fiery little lieutenant by the name of George Vancouver, and a good-natured fellow midshipman named Peter Puget.

Deptford supply depot on the Thames River where Vancouver's ships Discovery *and* Chatham *were outfitted.*

CHAPTER 3

The Vancouver Team

The sloop of war *Discovery*, a 340-ton vessel, was built in 1789 at the Thames River shipyard of Ramdall and Brant. She was purchased by the Admiralty before completion, to be outfitted for a voyage of exploration to the South Pacific. Her mission was to be an extension of the Cook expeditions[1] (1768-1779) which had yielded such a wealth of information about that vast area, and so many land claims for England. It was entirely logical therefore that command of the expedition was given to Captain Henry Roberts, with George Vancouver to be first Lieutenant, as both men had accompanied Cook on his second and third voyages.

The *Discovery* had almost completed fitting out for the voyage when a former British navy officer, John Meares, more recently a merchant captain trading between the Northwest Coast of North America and the Orient, delivered a letter to Parliament which had all the effect of a bombshell. He reported that at Nootka Sound, the Spanish had desecrated the British flag, seized the British ships and territory, and had imprisoned British seamen. That would have been an inflammatory message no matter what country had been the reported offender. With Spain, those were fighting words!

Parliament demanded instant vengeance against the ancient enemy. The response was the "Great Spanish Armament"—the assemblage of the largest fleet of warships in naval history up to that time. All other naval missions were dropped or put on "hold," including the voyage of the *Discovery* to the South Pacific. Captain Roberts was reassigned to the Caribbean and Vancouver rejoined Commodore Alan Gardner in the battleship *Courageux*. The *Discovery* was left at dockside in the Thames River under the charge of a recently promoted lieutenant, Peter Puget. There her first official service would be as a receiving ship for the reluctant "volunteers" rounded up by the pressgangs sweeping through the dockside taverns and byways of every port.

The repercussions of the Great Spanish Armament were felt on both sides of the Atlantic. George Washington had just been inaugurated as the first President of the United States when the trouble began. Spain demanded help from the fledging republic on the basis that she, together with France, had provided vital assistance to America in their recent war for independence. England, on the other hand, haughtily demanded permission to march troops through her former colonies to attack the Spanish forces in Louisiana. Washington took a firm position of armed neutrality, thus setting the pattern for his later advocacy of a "no foreign entanglements" policy.

The reaction in Spain was confusion and dismay rather than belligerency. King Carlos III had recently died, and his son, Carlos IV, was endeavoring to maintain the status quo with his father's program of enlightened development. The Malaspina expedition had just been dispatched to the Pacific to gain more

Maritime Museum, Victoria, British Columbia.

Portrait generally believed to be of Captain George Vancouver.

25

knowledge of the area where Spain was attempting to maintain its colonization "edge" over its other European competitors. A speck of land at Nootka, and what it believed to be an exaggerated claim from Meares, no doubt seemed insufficient cause to start another major war, particularly one it could not hope to win against such overwhelming British naval forces.

Spain sought a peaceful solution, and on October 28, 1790, signed a treaty known as the Nootka Convention. Under terms of the treaty, "Restitution was offered to England for the captures and aggressions made by the subjects of His Catholic Majesty, together with an acknowledgement of an equal right with Spain to the exercise and prosecution of all commercial undertakings in those seas, reputed before to belong only to the Spanish Crown." As the result of this conclusion, Vancouver wrote, "It was deemed expedient that an officer should be sent to Nootka to receive back in form a restitution of the territories on which the Spainiards had seized,...". Vancouver was promoted to the rank of Commander and given command of the *Discovery*, charged with carrying out that assignment.

Vancouver's plan for the expedition team was affected by one more "bombshell," this one exploding in the headquarters of Admiralty. News had just arrived of the mutiny on the *Bounty*, which had taken place in the south Pacific in 1789. Mutiny! The very word struck the fire of anger (and yes, fear) in the mind of every ship commander of the day. The inciting conditions were to be found in one degree or another aboard every ship. Crews, some having been dragged aboard by pressgangs, separated from home and family for years at a time, kept barely alive by "live" food and putrid water, punished by the lash for the slightest infractions, could easily sink into a mood of "nothing more to lose." Eighteenth century sea officers were given no training in diplomacy or interpersonal skills (certainly neither Bligh nor Vancouver), and a sadistic or even thoughtless captain or mate could easily push a habitually disgruntled crew over the limits of sanity. Even so, mutiny had seldom occurred when ships were sailing in company. Noting this fact, the Admiralty determined

that henceforth no single ship missions would be launched on multi-year expeditions. The *Discovery* would be accompanied by the armed tender, *HMS Chatham*, under the command of Lt. William Broughton. For good measure, the *Discovery* would carry a larger Marine detachment than normal, and the *Chatham*, too small to rate any at all, was assigned a Marine squad under a sergeant.

Vancouver thus had to complete the staffing and provisioning for two ships for a multi-year expedition. The magnitude of the task is indicated by the ship dimensions and the muster tables displayed on the

National Maritime Museum, Greenwich, England.
Lieutenant and Gunnery Officer. Sketch by Thomas Rowlandson, circa 1796.

Captain (later Vice Admiral and Baronet) Alan Gardner, Commodore in command of the West Indies station when Baker, Vashon, Puget and Vancouver served aboard his ship, Europa.

Zacharia Mudge, First Lieutenant on Vancouver's ship Discovery.

following pages. Vancouver was given the choice of a few of his officers, particularly the 2nd and 3rd lieutenants, and the (sailing) Master on the *Discovery*. He selected Peter Puget as his 2nd lieutenant and Joseph Baker as his 3rd lieutenant, based on his favorable fellow officer experience aboard *Europa*. Both had just recently completed their examinations for promotion to the rank of lieutenant. Vancouver may also have sought counsel on this matter from Commodore Gardner, whose favorable recommendation had been an important element in his selection for this new command. For the important position of Master, the highest warrant officer, Vancouver selected Joseph

Whidbey, with whom he had served in prior commands. Whidbey was one of the very few people Vancouver considered to have skills as a navigator equal to his own.

A brief resume for each of several key members of the expedition team will indicate the variety of skills and the level (or lack) of experience available for the tasks ahead.

The age and service of each individual is as of March 1791.

Captain George Vancouver—Age 34; Service 20 years, including duty in all oceans, major naval combat, and the 2nd and 3rd James Cook voyages of exploration. Vancouver was regarded as a superb navigator. This was his first command.

1st Lieut. *(Discovery)* Zachary Mudge—Age 21; Service 11 years, duty in Atlantic, assigned to *Discovery*

H.M.S. Discovery

Built: 1789 by Randall and Brent on the
   Thames River
Class: sloop-of-war
Rigging: ship
Deck: 96'
Keel: 79'
Breadth: 27' 3¾"
Length/breadth ratio: 4 to 1
Tonnage: 337
Guns: ten 4-pounders
   ten swivels
Later uses: bomb vessel, 1795-1808
   prison ship, 1808-1834
Destroyed: 1834, broken up at Deptford

Courtesy of the artist, Steve Mayo.

MUSTER TABLE OF HIS MAJESTY'S SLOOP THE *DISCOVERY*
BETWEEN 1ST APRIL AND THE 31ST MAY, 1791

COMPLEMENT 100

MEN'S NAMES	QUALITIES	AGE	MEN'S NAMES	QUALITIES	AGE
Geo. Vancouver	Capt.		Jos. Baker	3rd Lt.	
Rich'd Richard	Boat's		Wm. Wooderson	A.B.	19
Rich'd Collett	Gunner		Jos. Morgan	A.B.	23
Henry Phillips	Carpenter		Jno. Rogers	A.B.	20
James Gransell	Cook		Geo. Evans	A.B.	25
Widow's Man	A.B.		James Harris	A.B.	28
Robert Stephens	Mid.	19	Jno. King	A.B.	23
Edw'd Williamson	A.B.	31	Jos. Murgatroyd	Carp'r Mate	38
Chas. Mason	A.B.	24	Jn'o Davies	A.B.	27
W.M. Waller	A.B.	24	Rich'd Bown	A.B.	19
Geo. Hart	Qtr. Mr.	24	Jno. Willis	A.B.	25
Philip Butcher	A.B.	23	Donald McNeal	A.B.	20
Jn'o Lucas	A.B.	35	Thos. Spearer	Q'r M'r	26
James Hitchcock	A.B.	18	Jno. Cook	A.B.	21
Geo. Simpson	A.B.	18	Robert Barrie	Mid.	19
1 April '91	Corp'l		Wm. Milne	A.B.	27
E.C. Harris	A.B.	19	A.P. Cranstoun	Surg'n	
Arthur Crews	Mid.	22	Thos. Clarke	A.B.	18
Jn'o Noot	Bo. M'te	29	1 Feb. '91	Mid.	
Geo. Philliskirk	Bo. M'te	23	Thos. Manley	Mr's Mte.	21
James Drummond	A.B.	37	Humphrey Evans	Q'r M'r	30
Jno. Davidson	A.B.	21	Henry Hankins	A.B.	23
Jno. Evans	A.B.	19	Adam Mill	Surgeons 1, Mate	25
Jno. Thomas	A.B.	19	Alex. Bell	A.B.	24
Lewis Jones	A.B.	22	Wm. Underwood	A.B.	21
And'w Gibson	2'd M'r	27	Peter Puget	2nd Lieut.	
James Wilkinson	A.B.	21	Zac. Mudge	2nd Lieut. 15 Dec. '90	
Walter Dillon	A.B.	27		1st Lieut. 3 Jan. '91	
Jos. Whidbey	Master		James Bailey	A.B.	23
Jno. Campbell	A.B.	20	Thomas Taylor	A.B.	25
Jno. Carter	A.B.	22	Sam. Manning	A.B.	23
Jno. Nicholas	Mid.	19	4 Mar. '91	Bo. Mte.	
Jno. Barrymore	A.B.	22	Thos. Keld	Q'r M'r	29
And'w Macready	A.B.	20	Jno. Brown	Q. M'r	28
Fras. Brown	A.B.	27	James Englehart	Sailmaker	20
Jno. McAlpine	A.B.	22	Alex. Norval	Cook's Mte.	20
Wm. Patterson	Sailmakers M'te	29	Jno. Aisley Browne	A.B.	17
8 May '91	A.B.		Robt. Pigot	Mid.	16
Jno. Cummings	A.B.	21	H.M. Orchard	Clk.	31
Corn's Downey	Carp't Crew	18	Jno. Stewart	A.B.	17
Jno. McKinley	A.B.	19	G.C. Hewitt	Surg. 1st Mate	
Jno. Allen	A.B.	19	Jos. Mears	Surg. 2nd Mate	
Rich'd Henley	A.B.	30	Ben Reeve	A.B.	26
Edw'd Berry	Gun'r Mte.	23	Thos. Keld	Boat'n	
Isaac Wooden	A.B.	23	Jno. Monroe	Q'r M'r	28
Jno. Blake	A.B.	18	Edw'd Roberts	A.B.	18
Thos. Laithwood	Carp'rs Mate	26	Nath. Ridley	Cook	
Wm. Guy	A.B.	27	Jno. Roome	A.B.	26
Alex. Foord	Carp't Crew	19	James Butters	Gun'r Mate	38
Jno. Gobourn	Carp't Crew	23	V.V. Ballard	A.B.	19
Geo. McKenzie	Mid.	16	Fras. Griffin	A.B.	24
Spelman Swaine	Mr's Mte.	22	Jno. Ash	A.B.	30
Henry Humphreys	Mid.	18	3 Mar. '91	Armourer	
Jno. Sykes	Mid.	19	Jno. Willcocks	Corp'l Mast'r at Arms	27
1 Feb. '91	Mr's Mte.		Thos. Townshend	A.B.	
Stephen Man	A.B.	25	Honble C. Stuart	A.B.	16
James Green	Carp. Mte.	22	Honble Thos. Pitt	A.B.	16
Rod'k Betton	A.B.	25	Geo. Fox	A.B.	30
Jno. Mitchell	A.B.	25	Thos. Young	A.B.	19
Thos. Brown	A.B.	26			

Muster tables showing the men aboard H.M.S. Discovery, *from originals among the Admiralty Records in the Public Record Office, London. "A.B." means able-bodied seaman.*

MUSTER TABLE OF HIS MAJESTY'S SHIP THE *CHATHAM*, ARMED TENDER
BETWEEN THE 1ST DAY OF MAY AND THE 30TH DAY OF JUNE, 1791

COMPLEMENT 45 MEN

MEN'S NAMES	QUALITIES	AGE	MEN'S NAMES	QUALITIES	AGE
Wm. Robt. Broughton	Lieut. & Commander		Hawkins Lloyd	A.B.	22
James Hanson	2nd Lieut.		James Robinson	A.B.	21
James Johnstone	Master		Thomas Deacon	A.B.	19
Wm. Wager	Q'r Mt'r	23	David Munro	A.B.	18
David Dorman	A.B.	21	Geo. Rosewell	A.B.	18
Adam Brown	A.B.	17	Wm. Bennett	A.B.	22
Charles Maskill	A.B. afterwards Q'r M'r Mate	25	John Best	Cook	
John Messingham	A.B.	22	James Bray	Carp'r	
William Gamble	A.B.	22	William Nicholl	Surgeon Mate	
John Wilkinson	Q'r M'tr Mate	26	John Sheriff	Master's Mate	
Edward Bell	Clk.	20	James Wood Scott	Mid.	
Sandford Martin	Carp'r		John Miller Garnier	Mid.	
Wm. Gifford	Gunner		Wm. Le Meswier	M'r Mte. to 31 Mar. '91 then A.B.	
Wm. Walker 2nd	Surgeon		Henry Barfleur	A.B.	
John Rycraft	A.B.	24	Thomas Young	A.B.	20
Thos. Heddington	Mid.	15	James Etchinson	A.B.	34
Chas. Guthrie	Bo. Mte.	23	Edward Williams	A.B.	27
Thos. Miller	Q'r M'tr	45	Thomas Townsend	Q'r M'r after Sailmaker	27
Wm. House	Boats'n		William Willson	Q'r M'r Mate	25
Wm. Howard	Gun'r Mate	29	Aug's Boyd Grant	Mid.	18
John Rogers	Q'r M'tr Mate	35	Edmund Atkinson	M'r Mate	22
James Beckett	Carp. Mate	30	James Coote	A.B.	18
James Webster	Bo. M'te	35			

Muster tables showing the men aboard the Chatham.

H.M.S. Chatham

Built: 1788 at Dover
Class: armed tender
Rigging: brig
Deck: 65'
Keel: 53' 1³/₄"
Breadth: 21' 6"
Length/breadth ratio: 2¹/₂ to 1
Tonnage: 135
Guns: four 3-pounders
    six swivels
Sold out of the service: 1830

Courtesy of the artist, Steve Mayo.

31

Vancouver's ships Discovery *and* Chatham *shown departing England, April 1791. Painting by Steve Mayo.*

Courtesy of Mr. & Mrs. Michael Walmsley.

when it was under command of Roberts—no record of prior service with or under Vancouver. Family well connected politically.

2nd Lieut. *(Discovery)* Peter Puget—Age 25; Service 13 years, duty in Atlantic, Caribbean, and Mediterranean including major combat; served aboard *HMS Europa* with Vancouver who requested his assignment to *Discovery.*

3rd Lieut. *(Discovery)* Joseph Baker—Age 23; Service 10 years. See Chapter 2.

Sailing Master *(Discovery)* Joseph Whidbey—Age 36; Service over 20 years; previous duty as shipmate with Vancouver who regarded him as an excellent navigator.

Botanist (later also surgeon) Archibald Menzies—Age 37; Service over 10 years; Sir Joseph Banks, President of The Royal Society, regarded him as an outstanding botanist, and insisted on his assignment to the expedition.

Lieut. (and Commander of *Chatham)* William Robert Broughton—Age 29; Service over 15 years; *Chatham* was his first command; Captured by Americans at the Battle of Bunker Hill in Boston; No

known prior service with Vancouver, assigned to the expedition by the Admiralty.

Lieut. *(Chatham)* James Hanson—details not located.

Master *(Chatham)* James Johnstone—Entered navy as midshipman, most recent service aboard *Chatham;* During an earlier break in navy service, he had sailed the Pacific on a fur trading voyage.

Master's Mate *(Discovery)* Spelman Swaine—Age 22; Service 10 years; Passed examination for promotion to lieutenant in 1791.

Filling out the muster tables of midshipmen, sail makers, carpenters, able-bodied seamen, etc., was a group of very young men, few over 30, one-quarter under 20. All were regular service personnel, no pressgang "volunteers." A few were apparently selected for their collateral skills in sketching, an important part of recording the results of explorations. The invention of the camera was yet fifty years away.

In addition to the people listed on the muster tables, there was a young native of the Sandwich Islands, named Towereroo. He had been brought to England as an ethnic curiosity by a fur trading captain, had not adapted in any way, and was now being consigned to Vancouver for return to his native islands.

It was planned that a third ship would be dispatched to rendezvous with Vancouver either in the Sandwich Islands or at Nootka, during the second winter of the expedition. Supplies for the *Discovery* and the *Chatham* would thus be replenished, and further instructions, if any, would be relayed to Vancouver. Assignment of such a vessel was left to a later date, but it would turn out to be the *Daedalus* under the command of Lt. Hergest, about whom we shall learn more in a later chapter.

By March of 1791 the expedition was nearing readiness to depart. The *Discovery* had proceeded down the Thames to Dover Strait, and through the English Channel to Falmouth Bay, the designated rendezvous point. Stormy weather in the Channel had claimed the ship's first casualty when carpenter's mate, John Brown fell overboard and was drowned.

Chatham was undergoing some last minute repairs, and was delayed in arriving. After *Discovery* had spent ten days at anchor, Vancouver was reaching the "end of his rope," which was never very long in the first place. Finally, on March 31, Lt. Baker noted in his log, "Arrived His Majesty's Armed Brig, *Chatham*......begin getting ready for sea." On April 1, 1791, Baker noted further, "..at 4 (a.m.) light air and clear, weigh'd (anchor) and made sail under topsails, topgallant sails, and royals, set studding sails,......at 8, Pendennis Castle north, 4 miles...in company with *Chatham*, at noon, Lizard (Point) N.W. 4 or 5 leagues." Baker was viewing the last bit of England he would see for four and one-half years.

The route Vancouver had selected would take them south along the west coast of Africa to Cape Town, around the Cape of Good Hope, east across the Indian Ocean to New Holland (Australia), east to New Zealand, northeast to Tahiti, and finally north to the Sandwich Islands (Hawaii). The first port of call, April 28, was Tenerife in the Canary Islands. While the *Chatham* was adding more stone ballast to improve her sailing qualities, a general resupply of food and water

was carried out. Vancouver was able to obtain a generous supply of quality wine. These men, or at least the officers, did not intend to "live by sea biscuits alone."

The two ships anchored in False Bay, off the Cape of Good Hope on July 9. The ships were in serious need of repairs, in an amount calculated to require three or four weeks. Under those circumstances as many men as could be spared were given shore leave. In 1791, and for several years thereafter, the Cape of Good Hope colony was under Dutch control. It was a very popular waypoint for ships sailing to and from Europe and the Orient. Unfortunately, ships sometimes carried more than passengers and cargo, in this instance, disease. A large Dutch ship returning from Batvia in the East Indies, anchored in False Bay and delivered many of her crew to the local hospital, very ill and dying from a severe form of dysentery. The disease quickly swept through Cape Town and back to every ship in the harbor, including both *Discovery* and *Chatham*. Among the hardest hit on the *Discovery* was Cranstoun, the ship's surgeon. Vancouver recognized this as "a calamity of the most serious and distressing nature." He hastened preparations to put to sea, and on August 17, departed False Bay in company with *Chatham* and a number of ships carrying convicts to the recently established prison colony at Port Jackson, New Holland (Australia). Many of the crew remained indisposed for weeks; on September 6, Neil Coil, a marine, succumbed to the ailment, the only death due to contagious disease during the four and one-half year expedition.

The ships proceeded across the southerly and lonely reaches of the Indian Ocean, through latitudes now frequently referred to as the "roaring forties." On September 9 they passed tiny St. Paul and Amsterdam islands, which lie one thousand miles from the nearest island, and twenty-five hundred miles from the nearest mainland.

The afternoon of September 26 brought a most welcome sight—land, the southwesterly tip of New Holland. A two day leisurely sail along this southerly coast yielded the discovery of a well protected harbor, which Vancouver named King George the Third's Sound. The harbor offered a veritable treasure of the things they most needed at that moment, sheltered anchorage, fresh water, an abundance of succulent oysters, edible greens, and above all, quiet beaches where the still recuperating members of the crew could take their ease. With all this to offer and no record of prior discovery by Europeans, Vancouver promptly celebrated "taking possession of the area" in the name of the King.

The expedition remained in the area for nearly a month during which they began the surveying and charting activities that were to form such a major part of Baker's efforts. Menzies was also able to commence his work of collecting and identifying the flora and fauna of this land. No contact was made with the native population, except to see a few abandoned and very primitive shelters together with evidence that these were a nomadic people, accompanied by dogs.

Noting that the expedition was beginning to slip behind schedule, Vancouver reluctantly ordered preparations for sea. During the third week of October, they proceeded east toward New Zealand, passing to the south of Van Dieman's Land (Tasmania) on October 27. They arrived at Dusky Bay at the southwest corner of the South Island on November 2. Vancouver had visited this area with Captain Cook in 1773, and he wanted to complete some unfinished charting of this multi-fingered bay. While some of the crew were so engaged, others found the fishing to be excellent and the supply of evergreen tips to be just what was needed to brew a fresh batch of spruce beer. Day by day, both the physical and mental state of the crew was improving.[2]

The weather turned very foul, and departure became a trial to get the ships safely out of Dusky Bay and away from the stormy coast. They succeeded on November 22, and arrived at Tahiti December 29, 1791.

Enroute to Tahiti, Vancouver's memories of earlier visits to that much storied paradise must have stirred his concerns. As a young trainee with Cook, he had been there several times, the most recent in 1777. He was well aware that the warm, sultry climate, the even sultrier women, and their free-swinging life-style could combine to make the job of keeping a crew of sailors under control, nearly impossible. As they neared Tahiti, Vancouver also noted that virtually all of the ailing members of the crew now seemed fully recovered. He increased the frequency with which the crews were assembled for a reading of "The Articles of War," the military code. For good measure, he drafted a special order dated December 25, 1791, his only documented Christmas message to ship's company. The two page order was an attempt to discourage "officers and seamen" from the temptation to appropriate anything loose on the ships for use as trading stock in unauthorized bargaining for goods and "services." Penalties, including "..disrating..will be inflicted on every person who shall be found to embezzle, or be concerned in embezzling, or offering to trade with, any part of the ship's or boat's stores, furniture, etc....be these of what nature soever."

Upon landing, Vancouver was disappointed to learn that most of the acquaintances he remembered from 1777 had since died, and the few that remained had retired from active leadership roles. But the atmosphere was just as friendly as ever, and there was no difficulty in negotiating for space and assistance in making repairs to the ships and long boats. An abundant supply of hogs, fowl, fruit and vegetables was available in exchange for hand axes, brightly colored cloth, and miscellaneous trinkets.

Vancouver experienced another disappointment in learning that Towereroo, the Sandwich Islander, was of no help in bridging the chronic language translation gap. Whatever the source of the problem, it apparently didn't form a serious communication barrier for Towereroo. Smitten by the charms of the daughter of one of the chiefs, he jumped ship, and the two headed for the hills. It was a scene that might have been lifted right out of the musical comedy, "South Pacific." Vancouver was "mortified" at this potential break in harmonious relations. The chief was equally displeased, but limited his action to sending three extended family, royal brothers after the couple. They delivered

Towereroo to Vancouver several days later, as the expedition was preparing to sail for the Sandwich Islands. The parting was on most friendly terms, accompanied by one more of an almost continuous series of gift exchanges. Final departure from Tahiti was accomplished on January 24, 1792.

Vancouver took stock. He noted that it was now ten months since they had left England, and only now were they embarking on the serious business of the expedition. The time spent charting the south shore of New Holland and Dusky Bay had been contemplated as desirable "extras," subject to "conditions," but the hard core of the mission orders began with the directive to "continue the survey of the Sandwich Islands." The first port of call was Kealakekua Bay on the west side of the Big Island (Hawaii). As Vancouver remembered, this was a well sheltered harbor for making ship repairs, and a location where a fresh supply of hogs, fruit and vegetables was readily available. For him, it was also a place that held much darker personal memories which will be recounted in a later chapter.

Anticipating the same sort of free market activity as that in Tahiti, Vancouver ordered the rereading of his order forbidding the "embezzling, or offering to trade with, any part of the ship's or boat's stores, furniture, etc...". He also headed off a repeat of further problems with Towereroo. Tianna, a local chief with whom first contact was made on March 3, immediately saw an advantage in hiring a native Sandwich Islander who was familiar with the language and customs of Englishmen. A deal was struck, and Vancouver bade Towereroo farewell, promising to check on his welfare when he returned the following winter.

Tianna proved to be a veritable fountain of information on changes in the Islands since Vancouver's last visit with Cook in 1778-79. First, he was a deputy chief to Kamehameha, the King of the Island of Hawaii (and destined to be King of all the Sandwich Islands). Further, he was acquainted with Captain Meares, the Englishman who had stirred up the trouble at Nootka which was the main motivation for Vancouver's mission. In fact, Tianna had accompanied Meares on a trip to China, from which he had brought back many new treasures—including a supply of muskets and ammunition. It was with considerable apprehension that Vancouver and his officers listened to the account of wars between island chiefs, and even plans for further struggles for power. And it was doubly disappointing to learn that there had been no sign of the supply ship, *Daedalus*, with which Vancouver had hoped to rendezvous.

The expedition departed the Island of Hawaii on March 4, and proceeded at a leisurely pace to the islands of Ranai (Lanai), Morotoi (Molokai), Woahoo (Oahu), and finally, on March 8, to Attowai (Kauai). Passages along the shores of each of these islands provided Baker opportunities to recheck and fill in the partially completed charts from the Cook expedition.

Vancouver directed the ships to an anchorage in Whyteete Bay on the south side of Attowai Island, a place he remembered as providing the shelter and the beach space they would need to reload and make ready for sea. While these tasks were being accomplished, Vancouver was able to make contact with two Englishmen and one American currently residing on this Island. They were in the employ of an American named Kendrick, sometime fur trader, presently interested in collecting sandlewood for shipment to the Orient. They were able to further update Vancouver on recent events, which only deepened the melancholy he derived from his observations. The demeanor of these formerly happy, open-handed native people, had deteriorated to something between "distant civility" and outright distrust. He was now told that this change had been caused, in part, by the increasing numbers of misbehaved ship crews frequenting the islands, plus the recurring inter-island wars, made ever more deadly by the advent of firearms. Recent stories from the other islands even carried the report of an attempt by armed natives to capture a trading schooner out of Macao. Vancouver resolved to attempt an inter-island peace making effort on his planned return next winter. For now, it was time to get on with the main mission.

When the reloading operation was completed,

and after a brief stop at the nearby island of Oneehow (Niihau) for a supply of choice yams, the expedition set sail for the west coast of North America. It was March 16, 1792.

A month and a day later, and after a cautious approach through fog and rain, the ships made landfall in the vicinity of present Mendocino, California. They turned north, following the coast of North America, then designated by Englishmen as New Albion (New England). They expected to reach the Juan de Fuca Straits some 600 miles to the north. Enroute, on April 27, and in the vicinity of 46° north latitude, Vancouver noted that "..the mountainous inland country...descends suddenly...might be deemed low land...was the appearance of an inlet, or a small river....nor did it seem accessible for vessels of our burthen, as the breakers extend 2 or 3 miles into the ocean...". Thus did Vancouver fail to identify the mouth of the mighty Columbia River. It must be allowed however, that given the apparent risks of the approach, balanced against the importance of his main mission, Vancouver's judgement was correct.

In the afternoon of the next day, April 28, on failing wind and a strong on-shore current, the ships were anchored 3 miles south of Destruction Island, about 3 miles off the coast of the State of Washington. Little could anyone of the officers and crew, anticipate or even imagine the historic encounter which awaited them the following morning. (See Chapter 1)

CHAPTER 4

Charts and Charts and Charts

The orders issued by the Lords High Commissioners of the Admiralty to Captain George Vancouver, under date of March 8, 1791, charged him to accomplish four specific tasks on his expedition to the west coast of North America.

1. Anticipating his imminent departure from England on a route around Africa, to New Holland (Australia), thence to the Sandwich Islands (Hawaii), he was directed to remain there through the winter months. While there he was to continue the survey of the islands commenced during the third Cook expedition in 1778.

2. As soon as the weather was favorable, certainly by February or March of 1792, he was to proceed to Nootka (on the west coast of Vancouver Island) where he was to officially receive from Spanish officers the return of land and buildings reportedly seized from British Captain Meares in April of 1789. The return of the property had been negotiated with the King of Spain, but the details of the treaty were still being drafted and a final copy was to be forwarded to Vancouver by a follow-on supply ship.

3. Vancouver was to make a detailed survey of the coast of North America from latitude 30° north (approximately 200 miles south of San Diego) to latitude 60° north (the southerly coast of Alaska). Pieces of this vast coast line had been charted by others, but no one had made a complete survey of the total. The justification for such a monumental effort was the lingering hope that there might exist a channel or a series of rivers and lakes by which transport vessels could sail through North America to the Atlantic Ocean, thus obviating the long perilous voyage around Cape Horn.

4. While making the above described survey, Vancouver was to ascertain with as much precision as possible, the number, extent, and situation of any settlements made by any European nation, and the time when each such settlement had been first made.

A tall order indeed! The time necessary to complete the task was estimated at two years. The orders provided that during each winter the ships would retreat to the Sandwich Islands where the charting of those islands would be completed and the ships could be repaired.

Two of the four major missions described in the orders required extensive charting, and it was for this task that Lt. Joseph Baker had demonstrated special talent and would make a major contribution toward the overall success of the expedition. A systematic procedure for carrying out the surveying and charting missions was established within the first two weeks after Vancouver's squadron entered the Juan de Fuca Straits.

From the initial anchorage inside Dungeness Spit, on April 30, 1792, the *Discovery* and the *Chatham* were moved on May 2, about fourteen miles into the excellent harbor Vancouver named Port Discovery, now known as Discovery Bay. This location provided immediate answers to many of their needs, firm anchorage, protection from storms from any quarter, with the bonus of a stream of mountain fresh water entering the bay nearby. To the practiced military eye of Vancouver, the small island at the entrance of the bay also provided "protection of the port against all attempts of an enemy, when properly fortified; and hence I called it Protection Island." He landed on this island, climbed to its flat top, and in addition to gaining an excellent viewpoint, was rewarded in finding "an extensive lawn covered with luxuriant grass, and diversified with an abundance of flowers....gooseberries and roses."

The weather was most pleasant, and with the ships well situated Vancouver "indulged our people...with a holiday, for the purpose of taking some recreation and exercise on shore." Not to overdo it however, a survey party was immediately formed, to include Vancouver and Menzies in one of the long boats, Puget in command of a second, and Johnstone in command of a third. Each boat was manned by oarsmen, usually six, and was equipped with sails which could be put up if conditions were favorable. The boats were supplied with stores for five days, and each was equipped with a chest of small arms plus a swivel gun (small cannon) mounted in the bow. Lt. Broughton was left in charge of the ships, with a long list of

Vancouver's Journal.

A typical small boat and crew surveying the shore near the present site of Port Townsend, Washington. Sketch by Midshipman Sykes.

Discovery Bay. Protection Island in the foreground, Mt. Rainier on the distant horizon.

Sketch by Midshipman Sykes, showing Mt. Rainier in the distance and illustrating the type of sail rig used on the ship's small boats.

Vancouver's Journal.

maintenance items to be accomplished. Whidbey was assigned to set up the observatory tent on shore, in order to get a fix on the latitude and longitude of Port Discovery, and he was also to survey the bay and adjacent shorelines. More typically Whidbey would be out with the survey boats, most often in command of one. First Lieutenant Mudge and third Lieutenant Baker remained with the ship *Discovery*, overseeing repairs, with Baker also working with Whidbey on navigation and charting tasks.

The field expedition left the ships at five o'clock the next morning, and for the next several days surveyed the shorelines, the inlets and islands in the vicinity of the present city of Port Townsend (the bay named by Vancouver for the Marquis of Townshend) and extending south nearly to the end of Hood Canal, (named for the Right Honorable Lord Hood). After passing Port Townsend and upon entering the broad waterway Vancouver would name Admiralty Inlet, there came into view "..the round snowy mountain...which, after my friend Rear Admiral Rainier,

I distinguished by the name of Mt. Rainier." The survey was guided by an overall principle intended to insure that no possibility of the legendary "northwest passage" would be overlooked. The rule was to keep the known continental shore to the right, and to follow each inlet to the point where ocean going commerce could not be navigated. Where multiple inlets were encountered, such as to the south of Port Townsend, the task was divided among the boat crews, with some distant visible point designated as the next rendezvous. The survey procedure was as detailed in the current mariner's handbook, *"The New Practical Navigator"* by John Hamilton Moore (see Chapter 2). The following excerpt from the 1800 edition of the handbook details the procedure for surveying a coast or a bay:

The daily activities of the little squadron quickly took on a pattern of routine which would endure throughout the following three summer seasons. It was understood that daylight hours were to be fully used for the survey tasks. That meant that camp must be broken and supplies reloaded into the boats before sunrise.

To take a Draft of a Coast in sailing along Shore.

Excerpts from the New Practical Navigator, the standard mariner's handbook for the late 18th century.

HAVING brought the ship to the most convenient place from whence the principal points of the Coast or Bay may be seen, either cast anchor if it is convenient, or lie as steady as possible; or, if the coast is too shoal, let the observations and measures be done in a boat; then, while the vessel is in a stationary situation, take with the azimuth compass, or sextant, the bearings in degrees, &c. of such points of the coast as form the most material projections or hollows; write down these bearings, and make a rough sketch of the coast, observing carefully to mark the points whose bearings were taken with letters, for the sake of reference.

Then let the ship or boat run in a direct line along, which must be carefully measured by the log, or otherwise, one, two, or three miles, more or less, until she comes to a situation from whence the same points before observed can be seen again: there let the vessel lie as in the foregoing station, and again observe the respective bearings and leading-marks where two points or bearings, as mountains, churches, trees and houses, any two remarkable objects in one, in degrees, &c. of the same noted points, which are also to be wrote down, and a rough sketch of the coast should be also taken from this station, for which purpose prepare an observation table, in which write distinctly and regularly the several celestial observations, bearings, distances, measured by the log-line, the rocks, shoals, soundings, overfalls, races of tides, and other remarks that may be made along the coast; the table may consist of seven or 8 columns disposed in the following order:

Observations in Navigating the Coast——, from Cape——— to Point———,being ——— Miles, measured by the Log, the Course from Station I. to II. being S. ¼ W.

Remarks on the Tides and the Nature and Dimensions of Rocks, Shoals and Anchorage.	Bearings of Rocks, Shoals, and their estimated Distances, when on a line with the Points or Heads of the Coasts.	Bearings and Distances taken at these Distances.	Time and Distance sailed from Station I.	Bearings at Station I.	Meridian Altitude of ☉	Year, Month, and Day.
	Points and Heads. M.	Fath.	H. M. Mi.		D. M.	
This rock is dry at low water, and seemed 100 yards in length, from N. W. to S. W. a leading Mark to it, is.———		A.N. 5°W. 22 B.W. 20°S.	1 27 ¼ 11 45 ½			

In like manner proceed to the second Station, and so on, until the whole Survey is completed.

While the vessel is running the base line from station to station, an accurate appearance of the coast should be made, to do which let four expert persons be appointed, one to take the bearing exactly with an azimuth compass; one to oversee the running out of the log-line, and to keep an account of the ship's way, so as to be readily able to tell the distance run when required; the third to attend the heaving of the lead, to write down the soundings and bearings of one or two head points, or remarkable points of the coast, taking at each depth; the fourth a draftsman, to draw out the necessary bearings and distances, and delineate the figures and windings

Sea drawings, taken according to the foregoing precepts, befides the real ufe they are of, <u>cannot fail to recommend the young mariner, who furveys and conftructs them, to the notice of his Superiors.</u>

Note. The fextant will be found the readieft and moft correct inftrument to take the angles, by being held in an horizontal pofition, by which means any two objects not exceeding 120° may be brought into contact; it will not be amifs to take material points by the compafs, and intermediate ones by the fextant or quadrant.

EXAMPLE II.

This harbour was furveyed by bafe lines taken on fhore, which, when it can be done, is far preferable.

The bafe line AB 812 fathoms was taken, as by directions on the moft even fpot on fhore; now, beginning from the point A;

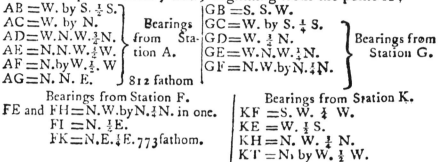

AB = W. by S. ½ S.   GB = S. S. W.
AC = W. by N.   Bearings GC = W. by S. ¼ S.
AD = W.N.W. ¾ N. from Sta- GD = W. ¼ N. Bearings from
AE = N.N.W. ½ W. tion A. GE = W.N.W. ¼ N. Station G.
AF = N. by W. ¼ W   GF = N.W. by N. ¼ N.
AG = N. N. E.   812 fathom

Bearings from Station F.   Bearings from Station K.
FE and FH = N.W. by N. ¼ N. in one. KF = S. W. ¼ W.
FI = N. ½ E.   KE = W. ½ S.
FK = N.E. ¼ E. 773 fathom.   KH = N. W. ¼ N.
            KI = N. by W. ½ W.
            NN = N. ¼ E.

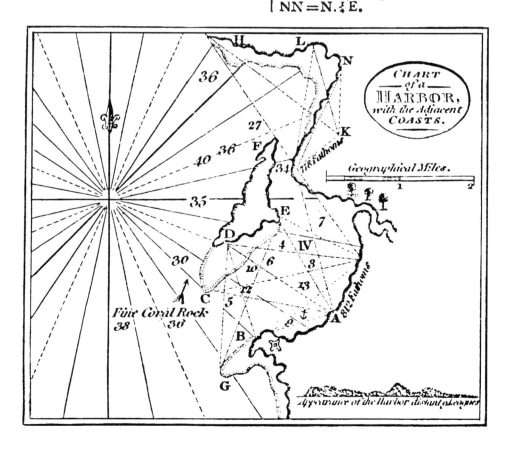

CHART of a HARBOR, with the Adjacent COASTS.

Geographical Miles.

Fine Coral Rock

Appearance of the Harbor diftant 3 Leagues

Portrayal of Vancouver and boat crew surveying in British Columbia waters.
Field data was used by Lt. Baker to prepare charts of the explorations.

Maritime Museum, Victoria, British Columbia.

Meal breaks were taken when the progress of the work and the availability of a favorable beach so indicated. The end of the workday came when it became too dark to take compass bearings or sextant sights, after which it might be necessary to row the boats another hour or two to reach a satisfactory camp site. So it went, rain or shine—stormy weather was only rarely considered cause to break early or hole up for a day, unless fog was also a problem. It was not unusual for crews to go for a week, soaked to the skin.

Menzies, the botanist (and ship's surgeon) was nearly always with one of the boat crews, surveying the flora and fauna of each new area, and assessing the capacity of the land to support agricultural enterprise. He collected seeds and seedlings of unfamiliar plants whenever possible. The madrona tree, so familiar in the Puget Sound area, was first identified by him, and thus named Arbutus Menziesia.

Every opportunity was taken to make friendly contact with the native people. Most of these efforts were successful, resulting in agreeable trade. The natives thus became an important source of supply of fish and venison to supplement the meager fare of salt pork and weevil ridden biscuits from ship's stores. The natives

around Discovery Bay had seemed strangely indifferent to the ships, due likely to their having seen either Eliza's ship or Quimper's which had earlier penetrated the Juan de Fuca Straits about that distance, but such was clearly not the case as the expedition continued.

The three boats completed the examination of Hood Canal and returned to the ships on May 15 to the great relief of their shipmates, since they were three days beyond the original plan. This was a problem often to be repeated. A boat crew sent out on a mission estimated to require three days or seven days, would frequently find it necessary to extend its survey by one or two days to get conclusive results—always with the consequence of generating alarm for the boat crew's safety back at the ships.

Vancouver was pleased to see the progress which had been made in repairing the ships, and he was anxious as ever to move on. He decided to send Broughton with the *Chatham* to the northeast to explore the several inlets which they could see in the distance across the Straits. The *Discovery* would be moved forward through the extensive waterways Vancouver had seen to the south of the entrance to Hood Canal, toward Mt. Rainier. Vancouver was also pleased to note the thoroughness of the work

An observatory tent similar to those set up on land to enable Vancouver, Whidbey and other late 18th Century mariners to make precise measurements of longitude. The subsequent development of accurate spring-wound watches and clocks made this cumbersome method of determining position unnecessary.

Courtesy of the National Maritime Museum, Greenwich, England

done in fixing the location of Port Discovery at 48° 02'30" north latitude, and 237° 22'19" east longitude. This had required the use of the equipment set up in the observatory tent, and the meticulous efforts of six or more of the officers and midshipmen in making 220 sets of 6 observations each, of the angular distance between the sun and the moon, followed by pages of trigonometric calculations for each set.[1]

As the junior officer aboard the *Discovery*, Baker was called on to perform one other task worthy of note, namely maintaining the record of punishments to the crew. This subject always evokes critical comment when judged against present day standards of military justice. The use of the lash as punishment for misbehavior, now seems to be unacceptable, even counterproductive, as a means of crew control. By way of explanation (not justification), the vulnerability of a ship, half-a-world

away from help, to the misdeeds of one individual, allowed such brutal discipline to be acceptable. After all, there were few privileges to be withheld from the spartan life of a lowly seaman as an alternative to corporal punishment. Taking as a sample, a one month period in late spring of 1792, Baker's log shows that the lash was ordered by the captain on seven occasions, to a total of nine individuals. Insolence to a superior officer or minor neglect of duty brought 12 lashes; drunkeness or repeated insolence, carried 24 lashes; and theft or neglect of important duty, earned 36 lashes. In most cases, the miscreant was not a brash young sailor, but rather one of the older seadogs in the crew.

In departing the vicinity of Port Discovery, Vancouver has left us many interesting descriptions of the area, some of familiar note and some in sharp contrast to the present condition. Example: "The

43

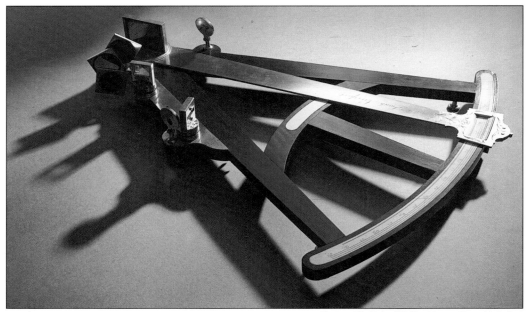

Portrayal of a boat crew departing the
ship, Discovery on a surveying
mission under command of Lt. Puget.
Steve Mayo, artist.

*Hadley quadrant, the type of instrument used by mariners in
the 18th Century to make astronomical measurements.*

Courtesy of the National Maritime Museum, Greenwich, England

region...seemed nearly destitute of human beings...also
had deserted the shores; the tracks of deer were no longer
to be seen;...animated nature seemed nearly exhausted;
and her awful silence was only now and then interrupted
by the croaking of a raven, the breathing of a seal, or the
scream of an eagle..". As to the land "regarded in an
agricultural point of view, I should conceive is capable of
high improvement, notwithstanding the soil in general
may be considered to be light and sandy. Its spontaneous
productions in the vicinity of the woods are nearly the
same, and grow in equal luxuriance with those under a
similar parallel in Europe;...the mildness of the climate,
and the forwardness of every species of plants, afforded
strong grounds to support of this opinion."[2]

The ships departed Port Discovery about noon
on May 18, 1792. By the following evening, the ship
Discovery had reached a suitable anchorage off the
southeast tip of present day Bainbridge Island.
Vancouver would later name this location Restoration
Point, on the anniversary of the restoration of the English
monarchy.[3] From this location it was possible to see
several branches of the waterway the *Discovery* had just
traversed. Two, one to the southeast and one to the
southwest, appeared of such consequence as to warrant
a full survey.

Vancouver ordered Lt. Puget to take two long
boats, and in company with Whidbey, Menzies,
midshipman Manby and twelve crewmen, survey the
southwest branch of the waterway. The expedition

44 *This K-3 chronometer was one of several spring-wound clocks carried on the
Vancouver expedition.*

One of the charts prepared by Lieutenant
Joseph Baker and included in Vancouver's
journal of the expedition. Discovery's path
is indicated on the chart.

Vancouver's Journal.

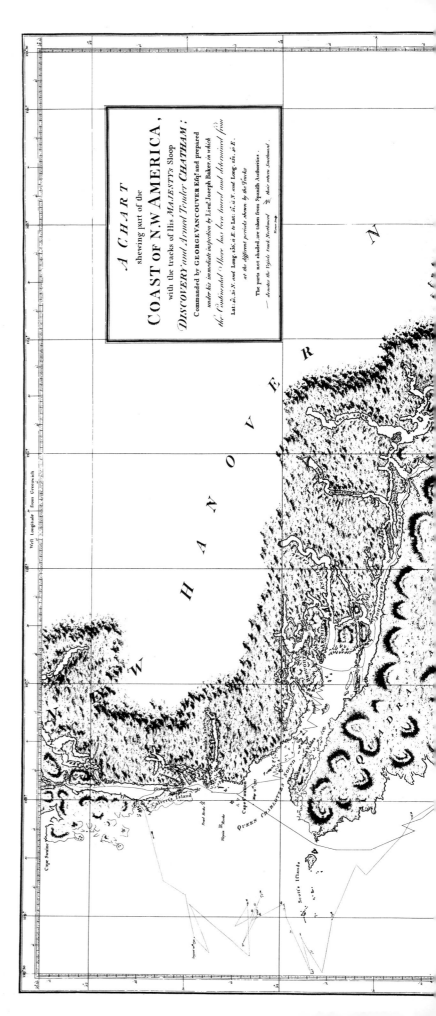

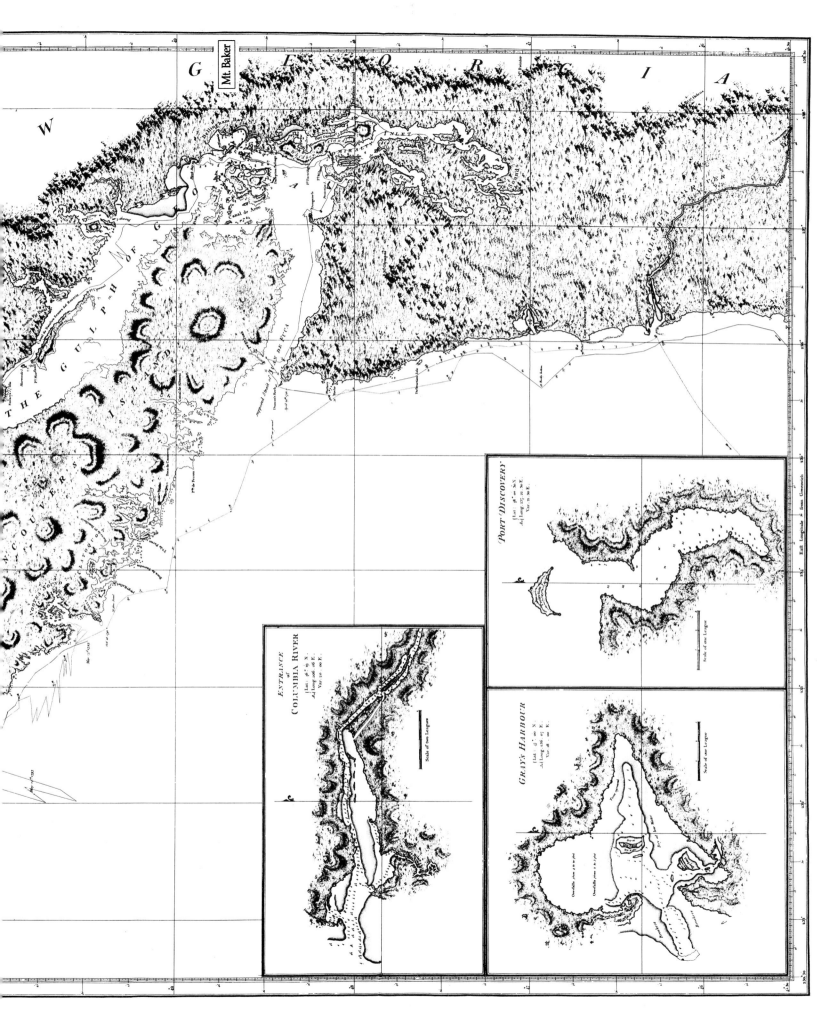

Mt. Baker

PORT DISCOVERY

ENTRANCE of COLUMBIA RIVER

GRAY'S HARBOUR

departed the *Discovery* at 4 o'clock the following morning, May 20, carrying supplies for five days. The plan was to follow the same procedures employed on the Hood Canal expedition. The result was the well documented survey which, within seven days, extended to every major waterway south of Restoration Point with such thoroughness that Vancouver ordered the area covered to be named Puget's Sound. Again, the survey took two days longer than planned, putting Vancouver in a more than usual frantic state. When Puget had not returned on the sixth day after departure, Vancouver ordered out another long boat and crew and launched a search up the southeast branch.

During the absence of Puget's expedition, the *Chatham* had rejoined the *Discovery* off Restoration Point. Before departing on his search for Puget, Vancouver left orders with Lt. Broughton that upon Whidbey's return, he should be transferred with one of *Discovery's* long boats to accompany the *Chatham* on a survey of the northwesterly passage from Elliott Bay (the present location of Seattle) and thence northeasterly (toward the present site of the City of Everett).

Puget, with Whidbey, did return to the *Discovery* about two o'clock in the morning of May 27. Vancouver returned two days later, having missed Puget's returning boats, but in the process he observed that the southeast and the southwest branches of the waterway they had pursued, actually rejoined about 15 miles south of Restoration Point, thus encompassing a rather large island. He named this Vashon Island, honoring his old friend and Lt. Joseph Baker's first skipper, (then) Captain James Vashon.

From Puget's report it was clear that he had exhausted any possibility of a "northwest passage" emanating from Puget Sound. The search would now be directed to the north.

Elliott Bay, now one of the busiest American seaports, is accurately shown on the chart Baker prepared, although Vancouver did not regard it as significant enough to give it a name. Aside from his designation of the southerly portion of this inland sea as Puget Sound, neither he nor Puget gave any permanent names to any of the many bays, inlets, islands, and headlands south of Vashon Island. The geographic nomenclature of that area was largely supplied by Wilkes as Commander of the 1841 survey from the United States Navy sloop-of-war *Vincennes* and the brig *Porpoise*.

The ships were now both moving north in stages interspersed with surveys from the long boats. Holding the continental shore on the right, and following the path of the *Chatham*, the *Discovery* passed Elliott Bay, reentered a short stretch of Admiralty Inlet, and then turned northeast into a very pleasant bay—pleasant that is except for the way they learned that its northern end was not navigable. The *Chatham* ran aground, due, Vancouver fumed, to the carelessness of her leadsman. Fortunately, the bottom was soft mud, and she was freed on the next tide change with no serious damage.

On Sunday, June 3, the ships anchored in the small bay on the eastern shore, known today by the Indian name, Tulalip. The early summer weather was clear and mild, and Vancouver was feeling magnanimous—he declared a holiday for all hands. He must also have been feeling possessive on behalf of his King, George III, whose birthday would be marked the following day. Vancouver's journal for June 4 notes, "..on which auspicious day, I had long since designed to take formal possession of all the countries we had lately been employed in exploring in the name of, and for His Britannic Majesty, his heirs and successors." His definition of the lands covered under this declaration was rather grand, extending north along the ocean coast from Mendocino, California to the northerly side of the Juan de Fuca Straits, plus all of the inland sea they had just surveyed, and including all the abutting and intervening lands north of latitude 45°, (say Salem, Oregon). Though thinly supported by the extent of the exploration and the lack of any occupation, this claim would, fifty years later, play an important role in the resolution of international boundaries.

For the moment, the declaration was made the centerpiece of a near comic-opera military pageant. Ship's company was mustered ashore; the English

Chatham *aground in Port Susan. Discovery in background.*

Artist, Steve Mayo. Courtesy of Mike and Penny Buse.

colors were raised to drum rolls and flourishes and a royal salute was fired from all the limited number of cannon aboard the two ships. Vancouver noted that ship's company "were served as good a dinner as we were able to provide them, with double allowance of grog to drink the King's health." That certainly assured the enthusiastic participation of all hands. We are left only to wonder at the reaction of the mild-mannered Indians with whom they had just been trading, and for whom this ceremony was a sort of sneak preview of things to come.

Vancouver completed the formal aspect of the declaration by naming the lands claimed as New Georgia, and the branch of the waterway by which they had arrived, Possession Sound. He also named the northwesterly branch, Port Gardner, in honor of Commodore Gardner, under whom Vancouver, Puget,

and Baker had all served. The northeasterly branch, lying along the east side of Camano Island, was named Port Susan, for the Commodore's wife. Lt. Baker duly added these new names to the chart being prepared.

On June 5, the ships resumed course to the north, moving in stages as the long boat surveys progressed. When the large body of land lying to the west of Port Gardner, was determined by the discovery of Deception Pass to be an island, Vancouver honored his steadfast navigator by naming it Whidbey Island. The *Discovery* moved through the San Juan Islands, which Lt. Broughton had previously surveyed in the *Chatham*. Continued favorable weather provided frequent views of Mt. Baker, for which they determined the latitude to be north 48°39'.[4]

By June 11, the ships anchored in Birch Bay, southwest of the City of Blaine. The long boats were

49

resupplied for seven days and departed in several directions to continue the survey. The next day, Vancouver, following a course to the north and then west from the ships, reached a prominent headland, which he named Point Roberts "after my esteemed friend and predecessor in the *Discovery*."

Vancouver and Puget rounded Point Roberts, took a northwesterly heading up the Straits of Georgia and over the next week would survey Burrard Inlet (Vancouver, British Columbia), Howe Sound, and Jervis Inlet, ranging as far as 130 miles from the ships. Whidbey departed the ships on June 13 to make a fill-in survey to the south of Birch Bay. He returned a few hours later with the startling news that he had seen "two strange sails" approaching from the south. The two small vessels anchored in Birch Bay during the night. In the morning, Baker joined Broughton in the *Chatham* and paid a visit on the new arrivals. They proved to be Spanish vessels, the one a small brig named *Sutil*, commanded by Dionisio Alcala Galiano, the other a modified schooner named *Mexicana*, commanded by Cayetano Valdes.[5] Their mission, like Vancouver's was to survey this coast in search for the northwest passage and to improve on the geographical location data gathered by an earlier Spanish survey. Galiano added the news that Captain Juan Francisco de la Bodega y Quadra, Commander in Chief of the Spanish Navy in Mexico and California, was now at Friendly Cove awaiting the arrival of Vancouver for a resolution of the Nootka settlement. After some thoroughly friendly discussion, the *Chatham* returned to its anchorage with the *Discovery*. Next morning the Spanish vessels followed the object of their pursuit to the north. After a successful but taxing expedition to the north, Vancouver and Puget returned toward the ships on June 22. They spotted two vessels at anchor along the south shore of the entrance to Burrard Inlet. At first thinking that the *Discovery* and *Chatham* had perhaps moved forward to meet them, Vancouver shortly recognized "that they were a brig and a schooner, wearing the colors of Spanish vessels of war." If Whidbey had been startled at first seeing these ships,

Vancouver noted "acknowledging that, on this occasion, I experienced no small degree of mortification in finding the external shores of the gulph had been visited, and already examined a few miles beyond where my researches during the (latest) excursion had extended..". Notwithstanding Vancouver's emotional shock, both groups of officers hit it off well, sharing a hearty breakfast. They agreed to share the work and the results of their survey efforts as they moved north in parallel, though Vancouver had some misgivings about this when he saw the small size and the generally poor condition of the Spanish vessels. Vancouver and Puget and their exhausted crews headed back toward *Discovery* and *Chatham*. Vancouver recorded that this meeting took place on June 22, 1792. For the same reasons explained in Chapter 1, Galiano noted in his log that it was June 21.

For the next three weeks the English and Spanish crews worked in concert as they moved north. To the labyrinth of waterways Vancouver applied many place names that have survived and become known to fishing and boating enthusiasts throughout the area—Desolation Sound, Point Mudge, Stuart Island, Menzies Bay, Johnstone Straits, to name a few.[6] As the survey moved north beyond Desolation Sound (and north of the present town of Campbell River), all of the crews encountered treacherous tidal currents in several of the passages. The pattern of the tides suggested the presence of a large body of water further to the north, or another opening to the sea. Mr. Johnstone, in command of one of Vancouver's long boat crews, convinced it was the latter, extended his assigned stay, and on July 10, reached a point in the vicinity of Port McNeill "from whence their expectations were gratified by a clear though distant view of the expansive ocean."

The word was quickly passed to both English and Spanish crews that the large land mass lying to the west of all their surveys of the past month was a major island. Vancouver would later instruct Baker to enter on the chart the name Quadra and Vancouver's Island.

It became increasingly clear that Galiano and Valdes were having difficulty keeping up with

Spanish ships Mexicana *and*
Sutil. *Mt. Baker in the distance.*

Spanish artist, Cardero. Museo Naval de Madrid.

Vancouver's crews, due, he thought to the miserable craft with which they were equipped. Agreeably, they exchanged sketches and survey data and parted company on July 13, with the expectation that they would meet again at Nootka. Vancouver continued north, even beyond the north tip of Vancouver Island, believing that pushing the survey forward as long as weather permitted was more important than an early appearance at Nootka.

The tedious routine continued during the next month, broken by short intervals of stark terror. Fog, rapidly changing tidal currents, and submerged rocks which defied even the most alert leadsman combined to vex the most intrepid mariner. On August 6, cruising through a particularly hazardous channel about ten miles north of present day Port Hardy, *Discovery* ran aground on sunken rocks. The tide was ebbing and as it receded, the *Discovery* took a frightful list to starboard. *Chatham* was anchored and all of her boats came to join the rescue effort. Top masts were immediately taken down, and together with every yard arm were used to shore up *Discovery*. Firewood, water, and rock ballast were thrown overboard to lighten her. Describing the miracle which made it possible to save her, Vancouver wrote, "Happily, at this time, there was not the smallest swell or agitation, although we were in the immediate vicinity of the ocean. This must ever be regarded as a very providential circumstance...". Certainly every mariner who has sailed those waters would agree. The returning tide refloated *Discovery* "without the least apparent injury." Baker noted "that in swaying into place the main top-gallant mast, the top-rope broke, by which means, John Turner (seaman) had his arm fractured." By the following noon, "the hold was restowed, and the ship, in every respect, ready again to proceed."

For most, that would seem to be enough excitement to last for some time, but such was not the lot of 18th century seafaring explorers. Six hours later, sailing in the same treacherous channel, but now several miles closer to the open ocean, the *Chatham* ran aground. Vancouver saw this situation as even more foreboding, for two reasons. There was now present a modest ocean swell which had the capacity to bounce the *Chatham* to pieces on the rocks. Adding to this, the crew had not had time to recover from the exertions of the past 48 hours in saving the *Discovery*. Vancouver dispatched Lt. Baker with all of *Discovery's* available

Menzies Bay, Vancouver Island, in British Columbia
waters. Vancouver named this bay in honor of the
botanist and surgeon on his expedition.

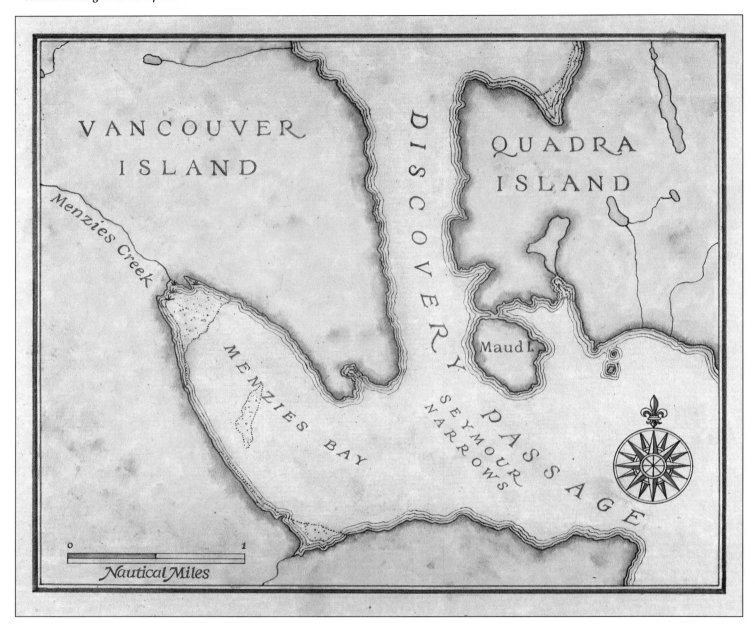

boat crews to the aid of *Chatham*. As darkness fell they repeated the exercise of taking down the topmasts to use as shores. Fortunately, when she struck, the ebb tide had partially past, so that the water level had little further to fall, and the flood tide was relatively few hours ahead. Baker reported to Vancouver the next morning that they had managed to refloat *Chatham* about half past one in the morning "...without the appearance of her having sustained any very material damage."

The undaunted squadron continued north through Queen Charlotte's Sound, and into Fitzhugh's Sound in further pursuit of the continental shore. The August weather began to deteriorate, suggesting that the surveying season would soon be coming to an end in this latitude. A sudden turn of events would end it even sooner than Vancouver had hoped. On August 11, a sheltered anchorage had been found in Safety Cove on the east side of Calvert Island. With the ships thus secured, the long boat expeditions were launched in the usual fashion. Within five days the boats were being driven back to the ships by most unpleasant weather. It was thus

Archibald Menzies, botanist and ship's surgeon on the Vancouver expedition, in his later years.

doubly startling when on August 17, "a brig was seen off the entrance of the cove, under English colors."

Baker launched a long boat and crew and crossed the cove to check her out. He reported back to Vancouver that she was the fur trader *Venus* out of Bengal, India, commanded by a Mr. Shepherd. Shepherd had recently visited Nootka and had a good-news/bad-news report for Vancouver. The good news was that the supply ship *Daedalus*, carrying new stores for *Discovery* and *Chatham*, had arrived at Nootka. The bad news, really horrible news, was that Lt. Hergest, commander of the *Daedalus*, his navigator, Mr. William Gooch, and one of his seamen, had all been murdered in the Sandwich Islands when they went ashore for wood and water. *Daedalus* was presently under the command of her sailing master, Mr. Thomas New who was awaiting Vancouver's orders. As soon as the boats could be gathered back to the ships, the squadron set sail for Nootka.

Discovery dropped anchor in Friendly Cove at Nootka on August 28, *Chatham* having arrived a few hours earlier. Vancouver was impressed with the level of maritime activity, four English and four Spanish ships at anchor, with Galiano and Valdes momentarily expected with the *Sutil* and the *Mexicana*. He was even more impressed by the supporting installations ashore—houses, warehouses, craft shops, a bakery with a new brick oven, etc. The formal presentation of credentials to the Spanish Commander, Bodega y Quadra, and arrangements for an exchange of ship's gun salutes was handled by junior officers. Vancouver appointed Lt. Hanson of the *Chatham* to be the new commander of the supply ship *Daedalus*. He further instructed Lt. Broughton to careen the *Chatham* on the harbor beach between tides in order to facilitate repair of any bottom damage resulting from her recent grounding in Queen Charlotte Sound. With these matters taken care of, Vancouver could now address his principle business with the Spanish Commander.

In the opening paragraphs of this chapter, reference is made to that portion of Vancouver's orders which authorized and directed him to receive from the Spanish Commander "the buildings and districts or parcels of land which were occupied by the subjects of His Britannic Majesty in April 1789...". This was part of the "Nootka Convention" negotiated between diplomatic representatives of England and Spain, as formalized on October 18, 1790. The Convention also stated that with respect to "the northwestern coasts of North America,..wherever the subjects of either of the two powers shall have made settlements since the month of April 1789,...any of the subjects of the other shall have free access." Vancouver understood the former provision to cover some substantial portion of Friendly Cove, and that the remainder would be covered by the latter provision, which would also cover any Spanish settlement north of San Francisco.

While awaiting Vancouver's arrival at Nootka for the past three months, Bodega y Quadra had spent his time reviewing this entire matter. He had gathered evidence from other ship captains, including the American Captain Gray,[7] who had knowledge of the 1789 situation, and from Maquinna, the highest ranking native chief in the region. Bodega y Quadra had reached the conclusion that Meares had grossly exaggerated his claims against Spain, that therefore he and Vancouver should reopen the case, and in effect renegotiate the

Discovery on the rocks in Queen Charlotte's Sound.

Sketch by Lt. Mudge.

terms of the Nootka Convention. Vancouver took the position that he was "not authorized to enter into a retrospective discussion of the respective rights and pretensions of the court of Spain or England....."

For over a month, the two commanders attempted to reach a mutually acceptable resolution, sometimes seeming to make progress, only to again revert to their original positions. On a personal basis the two individuals quickly formed a very warm friendship based on mutual respect. Though they apparently could converse in each other's language sufficiently well to handle routine navy business and banquet toasts to each other's Kings, their exchanges on this more delicate matter were mainly carried on in a series of notes, written and translated by a young midshipman from the crew of the *Daedalus* who was fluent and literate in both languages. The friendly tone of the exchanges is indicated by one of Bodega y Quadra's notes in which he said "that he derived the greatest satisfaction from finding a person of (Vancouver's) character with whom to transact the business of....Nootka." It is also indicated by the reciprocated banquets hosted on each other's ships, with native Chief Maquinna in attendance.

Finally, Vancouver and Bodega y Quadra were forced to recognize their need for further instructions from their respective governments. Also, each commander had plans to head south before the setting in of winter storms. A small Portuguese brig, the *Fenis And St. Joseph* was about to leave Friendly Cove for China. Vancouver procured passage for his First Lt. Mudge to return to England via the Orient, carrying a report to the Admiralty and requesting further instructions. With this change, Puget and Baker were advanced to First and Second Lieutenants respectively of the *Discovery* and ordered to prepare to depart Friendly Cove.

During the month of negotiations, Baker had been able to catch up on his charting work. This now

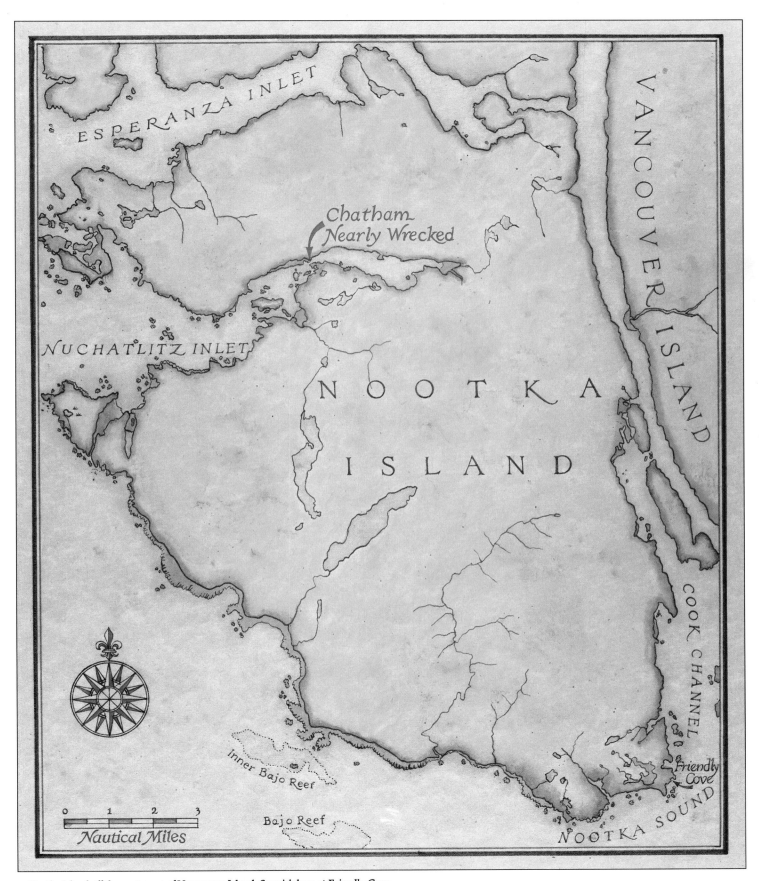

Map labels:

ESPERANZA INLET

VANCOUVER ISLAND

Chatham
Nearly Wrecked

NUCHATLITZ INLET

NOOTKA ISLAND

COOK CHANNEL

Friendly Cove

Inner Bajo Reef

Bajo Reef

0 1 2 3
Nautical Miles

NOOTKA SOUND

Nootka Island off the west coast of Vancouver Island. Spanish base at Friendly Cove.

*Friendly Cove, location of Spanish naval base (1789-1796). Focal
point of the British/Spanish dispute which Vancouver and
Bodega y Quadra endeavored to resolve.*
The Province of British Columbia.

made it possible for Vancouver to make good on a promise to give a copy of their surveys to Bodega y Quadra. In turn, Quadra reciprocated with copies of charts he had obtained from Captain Gray showing the paths by which the American had entered both Gray's Harbor and the Columbia River in the previous May, following his contact with Vancouver's ships off Destruction Island.

Bodega y Quadra suggested that he and Vancouver rendezvous at Monterey, California for a continuation of their discussions, after which he departed Friendly Cove aboard his ship *Activa* on September 22. After completing repairs to the *Discovery* and the *Chatham*, and finishing the transfer of supplies from the *Daedalus*, Vancouver followed on October 12.

Relieved, for the moment, of the need to focus on the Nootka Convention matter, Vancouver shifted his attention to planning the reexamination of the coast of the land he had named New Georgia, as they set a course south. He was not about to permit the continuation of the professional embarrassment that he (and several other captains) had missed the entrances to Gray's Harbor and the Columbia River. On October 18, having identified the landmarks on Gray's chart, Vancouver ordered Whidbey to assist the *Daedalus* in entering and examining Gray's Harbor. The next day, having reidentified Cape Disappointment with which they were familiar, Vancouver ordered Lt. Broughton in the *Chatham*, to lead into the supposed river just to the south, hopefully finding a break in the surf which appeared from the sea to have no such opening. Vancouver followed in the *Discovery*, but "We however soon arrived in three fathoms, and as the water was becoming less deep, and breaking in all directions around us, I hauled to the westward (seaward) in order to escape the threatened danger." *Discovery* anchored off shore with the crew in a state of considerable apprehension as to the safety of the *Chatham*. The next morning was calm and fair, and though the breakers appeared ominous, they were delighted to see *Chatham* anchored beyond in the river, and were able to exchange signals. The clear weather also permitted a view of yet another "high

round snowy mountain....(Vancouver)..distinguished by the name of Mount St. Helens."

After one more precarious and fruitless attempt to take *Discovery* across the bar into the river, Vancouver abandoned the venture, concluding (erroneously) that "My former opinion of this port being inaccessible to vessels of our burthen (size) was now fully confirmed....". *Discovery* put to sea and resumed her course to the south. Broughton kept *Chatham* in the river for over two weeks, during which time he extended a long boat survey up river a considerably further distance than Gray ventured. Broughton favored a number of his shipmates in naming various features of the river geography, including a large island for Puget and a group of small islands for Baker.

*Maquinna, a major chief of the Nootka Indians in the 1790s.
Sketch by a Spanish artist.*

Vancouver sailed down the coast of California, and after a short visit at the San Francisco mission, arrived at the then famous Port of Monterey Bay on November 25. *Discovery* was shortly joined by *Chatham* and *Daedalus*. Several Spanish ships were at anchor including the brig *Activa* flying Bodega y Quadra's broad pendant. Quadra had taken up residence at the Governor's house in the Presidio, from where he had issued orders that everything be done to assist and accommodate Vancouver and his officers and crew.

Quadra informed Vancouver that upon his arrival from Nootka, he had received orders from the Spanish Court, indicating a desire for accommodating British interests in the conduct of Spanish business at its various stations on the west coats of North America. They were both encouraged to believe that their respective sovereigns were ready to resolve any misunderstanding which might remain with respect to the Nootka Convention. With the hope of confirming the concurrence of the Admiralty in this resolve and obtaining the specifics of any new understanding, Vancouver proposed that he send Lt. Broughton to England via the fastest possible route, with appropriate dispatches and a complete report of his progress to date. Quadra agreed without hesitation, and invited Broughton to accompany him on his forthcoming voyage to the Spanish navy base at San Blas on the west coast of Mexico. Quadra would arrange transportation from there, overland across Mexico, and thence via ship to Spain and to England. Broughton packed his sea chest.

In his journal notations on these proceedings Vancouver again expressed the most favorable impressions of Bodega Y Quadra. He found him to be ever good humored, helpful but effective in all of their dealings, an attitude Vancouver would later learn, could not always be counted on in Spanish colonial administrators. Quadra was born and raised in Peru when it was a Spanish colony and that experience may have given him a desire for a less rigid style. Still, Vancouver noted that "To the reverence, esteem, and regard, that was shewn Senior Quadra by all persons and on all occasions, I must attribute some portion of the respect and friendship we received...".

Many tasks and new arrangements now had to be completed. The ships needed repair, as always, and a resupply of livestock and fresh food. On December 29, Lt. Hanson in command of the *Daedalus*, was ordered to depart for Australia. In preparation for the departure of Broughton with Quadra, Vancouver placed Lt. Puget in command of the *Chatham* and moved Lt. Baker to first lieutenant of the *Discovery*, though he made these promotions "acting," since he expected Broughton to somehow return, and rejoin the squadron.

A seafaring explorer had ever to be the optimist.

Friendly Cove, Nootka Sound. Sketch by Midshipman Humphries.

Vancouver's Journal.

CHAPTER 5

Aloha—Alaska

The *Discovery* and the *Chatham* departed Monterey for the Sandwich Islands on January 14, 1793. For the first three days they sailed in company with Quadra's ship, the *Activa*, which was enroute to San Blas, with Lt. Broughton as a passenger. On the fourth day, before taking sharply different courses, the ships hove to and the officers gathered aboard the *Discovery* for a parting dinner. It was one of those special occasions which again demonstrated the warm personal relationship that had developed between the two commanders. It would be the last time they would ever meet.

The *Discovery* and the *Chatham* reached the Sandwich Islands on February 12. Vancouver ordered the resumption of charting the coast of the big island, Hawaii. *Chatham* circled the east and south shores, *Discovery* proceeded along the north and west sides. They rendezvoused at one of the best harbors on that island, Kealakekua Bay. For Vancouver, this was a place of dark and haunting memories of that day, February 14, 1779, when he had been here, involved in the skirmish during which Captain James Cook was murdered. Every man present on that sad day must have wondered what he might have done to have avoided the sorry outcome.

It was under Cook's tutelage that Vancouver had learned and perfected his recognized skills as a navigator. It was these same skills which, in large measure, had earned him command of this expedition. Little wonder that he insisted on the highest standards of practice in gathering and charting the data which traced their path.

While Baker advanced the charting of the islands, amidst his duties as acting 1st Lieutenant, Vancouver was busy renewing the acquaintances of the few elder native leaders who remembered him from the "Cook" days. He learned that the intrigues and inter-island wars which had plagued this "island paradise" in the past, still continued. His efforts as a self-appointed peace-maker kept him busy, and the contacts he thus developed enabled him to pursue the answer to the murder of his supply ship's officers, Lt. Hergest and Mr. Gooch, during the previous summer. The answer to this mystery was provided in the course of a chance meeting with an American, James Coleman, one of three men who had earlier jumped ship from Kendrick's fur trading expedition and taken up residence with the natives. Coleman provided the story that Lt. Hergest, disregarding advice to the contrary, had landed on the northwest shore of the island of Oahu to replenish the water supply. The party was attacked by a band of renegade natives, who captured Hergest, Gooch and one seaman, all of whom were later murdered and dismembered for distribution as trophies. A strong complaint registered with the friendly chiefs in the Waikiki area resulted in the round-up of three supposed "villains." These were tried and convicted under a procedure combining native and King's justice. The death sentence was promptly carried out in a manner calculated to make an appropriate impact on the local population. In a canoe located offshore from the present day Waikiki resort area, and with a large gathering of the population on shore, a local chief blew their brains out with a borrowed pistol. Vancouver proposed that the bodies be hung for local viewing for several days, but the chiefs vetoed the idea as being contrary to local religious rites, offensive to the priesthood.

On a more pleasant note, Vancouver was able to complete a mercy mission he had undertaken at Nootka, as they had departed Friendly Cove the previous October. He had been approached by the captain of a British fur trading ship, *Jenny*, recently from the Hawaiian Islands. Captain Baker (no known connection to the family of Lt. Joseph Baker) related how after departing the islands, he had learned that his crew had enticed aboard and trapped two native girls, one fifteen, the other nineteen. The captain had immediately taken the girls under his personal protection. He was determined that they not fall prey to being sold as slaves to the Nootka natives, a fate which had been reported in other cases. Captain Baker had no plans for the *Jenny* to return to the Hawaiian Islands soon. Upon learning of Vancouver's itinerary, he asked that the girls be returned home aboard the *Discovery*. Vancouver, particularly repulsed by the slave trade

A CHART
of the
SANDWICH ISLANDS
as Surveyed during the Visits of His Majesty's Sloop
DISCOVERY *and Armed Tender* CHATHAM
Commanded by GEORGE VANCOUVER Esq.
in the Years 1792 1793 & 1794 ·
and prepared under his immediate inspection by
Lieut. Joseph Baker.

Vancouver's Spelling	Present Spelling
Owyhee	*Hawaii*
Mowee	*Maui*
Tahoorowa	*Kahoolawe*
Ranai	*Lanai*
Morotoi	*Molokai*
Woahoo	*Oahu*
Atooi (and Attowai)	*Kauai*
Oneehow	*Niihau*
Karakakooa	*Kealakekua*
Whyteete	*Waikiki*

possibility, had agreed to protect and return them. Completing that commitment now presented unforeseen problems. Exposure to the British and Spanish customs at Nootka, and European style clothes at Monterey had quite caught their fancy. But these newfound customs and habits were not well received by the Sandwich Island elders. And the idea of women eating with, rather than after men, was an absolute taboo. Vancouver was finally to negotiate a "reentry" arrangement with a chief on Atooi Island (now Kauai) including promises that the girls would not be punished for their innocently acquired new manners.

It was now mid-March 1793. Important progress had been made on the charting of the Sandwich Islands, with Puget and Whidbey shouldering the brunt of the field work, and Baker concentrating on the drafting of the charts. It was time to start thinking about returning to the North American coast to continue the explorations to the north.

A new factor caused a sudden acceleration of the schedule. A diving survey of the *Chatham's* bottom revealed the urgent need for repairs. Much of the copper sheathing had been lost in the occasional groundings, and the hull was leaking. This called for the tedious process of beaching the vessel, rolled first to one side, and then the other so that a renewal of the tarring and sheathing could be completed. However, that operation required a tide change of a magnitude never available in the Sandwich Islands.

Vancouver ordered Lt. Puget to set sail immediately on the 3,300 mile direct course to Nootka. The goal was to reach the sheltered harbor at Friendly Cove where there was ample change of tide to facilitate careening the ship for bottom repair. The route would almost certainly pass through the region of continuing winter storms in the north Pacific Ocean. And with that threat overcome, there would be the hazards of approaching the fog-shrouded and unmarked rocky west coast of Vancouver Island, an area which had become a cemetery of ships even after the provision of navigational aids. *Chatham* departed Owyee March 15, arrived at Nootka Island nearly a month later where she

mistakenly entered Nuchatlitz Inlet just north of Friendly Cove, and was nearly wrecked. However the gamble paid off when Puget was able to work *Chatham* into Friendly Cove, make the necessary repairs, and sail north to the appointed rendezvous with *Discovery*.

Meantime, Vancouver and Baker had reached Cape Mendocino (California) via a more southerly, and somewhat more comfortable route, and thence sailed north to Friendly Cove, arriving on May 20, 1793, after Puget and the *Chatham* had left. Vancouver learned that Salvador Fidalgo was currently in charge of the Spanish base, but was about to be replaced, and would soon be departing for San Blas. Fidalgo had no news from England for Vancouver, but he offered to carry any dispatches Vancouver wished to send to England via San Blas. Vancouver accepted this welcome offer and prepared a report of his progress for delivery to the Admiralty in London.

Vancouver departed Friendly Cove on May 23, and three days later met Puget with the *Chatham* near Point Menzies in Fitzhugh Sound. The business of charting the coast to the north was resumed with dispatch. Day after day, with rarely a break, Puget, Whidbey, Johnstone, Swaine, and often Vancouver himself left the ships with long boat crews to explore the maze of coves, inlets and fiords which constitute the northwest coast of North America.

These tours often lasted a week, occasionally more. As before, they used all the daylight hours for the business of exploring, which meant they were up before daybreak, and often rowing after dark to reach a campsite or return to the ships. Days on end, in fair weather and foul, with meager rations and no change of dry clothes, required a special devotion to the task. Occasionally there was the added threat of natives made hostile by the abuses of some of the fur traders who were beginning to reach the area. As the surveys of each area were completed and the long boats returned to the ships, the ships were moved forward to the next secure anchorage and the process repeated.

The survey data thus collected became the raw material from which Lt. Baker prepared the charts which were to become such an important part of expedition record. No one who has not participated in the task of reducing field survey notes to finished documents, can fully appreciate what a tedious and frustrating job that can be. No matter how well organized the data recording procedures nor how well intended the survey crews, the inevitable result was a collection of damp triangulation data sheets, finger-stained sketches of waterways, with some distances measured and some estimated. And always there would be those critical extra notes scribbled on limp paper which had been crumpled up in a shirt pocket for several days. It was Baker's special task to convert this mass of field data to first preliminary and then final charts. The preliminary charts of each area had to be fixed in latitude and longitude so that they could be integrated into the final regional charts which are part of Vancouver's Journal. His standards of accuracy for this latter step required that, particularly for the cumbersome lunar distance method of determining longitude, the accepted figure was the average of five or six individual's work, with each participant taking from twelve to twenty astronomical observations using a quadrant (similar to a sextant). Baker, Puget, Whidbey, and Vancouver were frequent participants in this critical step. Younger midshipmen were also included as part of their training. Also, it was this same process for determining longitude that was used as a basis for gauging the accuracy of the spring wound clocks.[1]

Weeks of the charting process blurred on, one into the next, with the routine broken only by events which were not always welcome. In mid-June, on one of the long boat excursions under the command of Mr. Johnstone, several of the crew were made violently ill after eating some contaminated mussels. They were "seized with numbness about their faces and extremities...attended by giddiness." One of the crew recognized the symptoms from a previous experience in England. The simplest field remedies available, such as inducing vomiting, were promptly applied. But for Able Seaman, John Carter, age 24, from Mitcham, no remedy could be found; he died within an hour. Vancouver

commemorated the man by designating Carter's Bay located at latitude 52° 48' North, longitude 231° 42' East. He designated the location of this sorry event as Poison Cove on "Muscle Canal."

Equally descriptive names were used to designate Traitor's Cove and Escape Point, where on August 12, a party of natives under the leadership of a woman who used her "turbulent tongue.....to compel the men to act with hostility," nearly ended in disaster. The approach of these natives, first presented as an offer to trade, was suddenly turned to an ugly attack on long boats carrying Vancouver, Puget, Menzies, and the usual crews. Only the most steadfast conduct of boat crews, and finally the firing of weapons which Vancouver reluctantly ordered, caused the natives to back off. In the melee, two of the crewmen were wounded by spears, one nearly mortally. He, Able Seaman, Roderick Betton, from Glasgow, was recognized by Vancouver with the naming of Betton's Island.

Vancouver continued his practice of recognizing individuals in the naming of bays, headlands, canals, etc., dividing the honor between British personages of prominence and members of his officers and crewmen whose performance met his high standards. Only rarely was anyone so recognized more than once. Lt. Baker was so honored on September 8, 1793, with the designation of Point Baker, at the northwesterly tip of Prince of Wale's Archipelago (now Prince of Wales Island). This was as far north as the expedition would go in 1793. Vancouver was no doubt expressing his approbation for the steadfast manner in which his First Lieutenant had "held the fort," much of the time in charge of the Discovery while most of the other officers were away in the long boats, and meantime preparing the accumulating set of superb charts to document the accomplishments of the expedition.

Point Baker is located at the northwesterly foot of Mount Calder, which is about 100 miles northwest of the present city of Ketchikan, Alaska, and approximately the same distance southeast of the Russian colonial capital, now Sitka, Alaska. Vancouver named an adjacent bay, Port Protection, and a nearby island, Conclusion. The conclusion of coastal surveys in this latitude was certainly indicated by the increasing frequency and duration of high winds and stormy seas. *Discovery* and *Chatham* departed on September 21, sailing for Nootka via the open sea route along the west coast of the Queen Charlotte Islands. They arrived in Friendly Cove on October 5.

The Spanish base at Nootka was now under the command of Senior Saavadra, who informed Vancouver that there had been no news either from England by sea or Spain via San Blas, on the matter of resolving the dispute over control of Friendly Cove. After three days Vancouver ordered a departure for Monterey.

On October 25, they crossed paths with the supply ship, *Daedalus* returning from Australia with badly needed stores for *Discovery* and *Chatham*. But when they entered Monterey Bay, intending to reload the ships, Vancouver was stunned by a distinctly chilly reception from the Spanish authorities. An oafish young infantry officer, Captain Arrillaga, acting as Governor, claimed lack of authority to receive foreign ships except on an emergency basis. Refusing to be bound by the past courtesies of Senior Quadra and others, Arrillaga stipulated unworkable limitations on Vancouver. Vancouver broke off any further negotiations, stating that he would depart for the Sandwich Islands where he had "little doubt that the uneducated inhabitants would cheerfully afford us that accommodation which had been unkindly denied us at Monterrey." *Discovery*, *Chatham*, and *Daedalus* sailed the next day, November 5. They proceeded south, making brief stops at Santa Barbara and San Diego, where they were again to learn that there was no news from England.

After an uneventful voyage, Vancouver's squadron arrived in the Sandwich Islands on January 8, 1794. The first landing was made on the northeast side of Owyhee, where Vancouver and King Kamehameha were mutually pleased to meet and renew their friendship. The ships proceeded around the southeasterly and west shores to Kealakekua Bay. Here they again found both the sheltered harbor and the ready welcome needed to facilitate the transfer of stores from the supply ship, *Daedalus* to *Discovery* and *Chatham*. With completion of this operation, *Daedalus* departed for Australia on February 8, 1794.

Vancouver permitted a somewhat more relaxed atmosphere for the crew than on the previous visit to the Islands. Some charting work remained to be done, but it was in the nature of completing missing pieces rather than any major new projects. The ships needed repair, as always, but the crews were not pressed for time to complete the tasks which were within their capabilities. As a consequence, the previously stringently limited shore leave policy was liberalized.

Lt. Baker and Menzies took advantage of the situation by organizing a small party to climb Mowna Roa (Mauna Loa), at 13,680 feet, the second highest mountain in the Islands. Mr. Menzies had failed in a previous attempt to scale this peak, and was anxious to find a better approach. They started out on February 6 with the assistance of local guides. The climb proved to be a formidable challenge, for they did not return until February 21.

During this period Vancouver found time to resume following one of his favorite interests, namely the political intrigue of the native power structure. He offered his advice and counsel on resolving disputes among the various leaders, which was rather well received. He even offered to mediate an altercation between King Kamehameha and his favorite wife, the Queen, which was, at first, rebuffed. Vancouver had great respect for these people, noting that, "our reception and entertainment here by these unlettered people, who in general have been distinguished by the appellation of savages, was such as, I believe, is seldom equalled by the most civilized nations of Europe." And the respect was reciprocated, based apparently on the King's appreciation of the disciplined and helpful behavior over the past three years of Vancouver's men, in general contrast to the rowdy behavior of the fur trade crews who were frequenting the Islands in increasing numbers. Vancouver even noted that the King's priests were including in their prayers, "the welfare of His Britannic Majesty."

During previous visits to the Islands, Vancouver had planted in the King's thinking the advantages of affiliation with His Britannic Majesty. Vancouver continued to promote this concept subtly, but with persistence. Finally on February 25, 1994, after the unanimous approval of his affiliated Chiefs, and at a ceremony convened on the deck of the *Discovery*, King Kamehameha "ceded the island of Owhyee to His Britannic Majesty, and acknowledged themselves to be subjects of Great Britain."

Vancouver was ecstatic. But, it would be several years before King Kamehameha had extended his control to the remainder of the principal Hawaiian Islands. More important, by the time Vancouver returned to England amidst the Napoleonic Wars, neither the Admiralty, nor Parliament, nor His Britannic Majesty could find time or reason to pursue the matter further.

Discovery and *Chatham* made their final departure from Owyhee on the following day, February 26, 1794. They proceeded along the northerly coasts of Mowee (Maui), Morotoi (Molokai), and Woahoo (Oahu), completing the charting and making few landings. Then on to Atooi (Kauai), from whence they took final leave of the Sandwich Islands on March 14.

Vancouver's plan for the coming season was to start the surveys at Cook's Inlet (near present day Anchorage, Alaska), proceeding thence east along the southerly coast of Alaska to Port Conclusion, where the previous year's survey had ended. This plan required that they head straight north across some 3,000 miles of the roughest winter seas of the Pacific Ocean. Even as the ships were departing, Puget reported that the *Chatham* was very "crank," meaning that it was inclined to list one way or the other. The two ships became separated after the first night, and would not rendezvous again for more than seven weeks, until May 7. The route north had fortunately avoided the most severe weather of which the north Pacific was capable. This was doubly so for the *Chatham*, which could proceed only under reduced sail. The previously reported listing was found to be caused by even greater than normal leaking; at one point she had shipped as much as four feet of water, requiring constant operation of the hand pumps.

The *Discovery* had made good progress north, making landfall at Tscherikow's (Chirikof) Island, southwest of Kodiak Island, on April 4. Within three weeks they had sailed from the tropical paradise of the Sandwich Islands to the frosted decks, the icy winds, and the gray snowy skies of Alaska. But not a moment was lost in resuming the surveys. Vancouver was in possession of Captain Cook's chart of the area, a chart he had taken part in making when he was present on Cook's third voyage in 1778. The first and most important step in this season's work was to trace Cook's Inlet (he had called it Cook's river) to its most northeasterly limit that represented the last possibility of a "Northwest Passage" to Hudson Bay. For this important phase Vancouver took a direct part in the long boat surveys, with Whidbey still leading the most arduous excursions. Baker remained in charge of the *Discovery* during Vancouver's absences and kept up the charting. By May 5, Whidbey and his crew had reached what was clearly the upper end of the inlet. Near that point he was forced to camp on a shore surrounded by chunks of ice.

When Whidbey returned to the *Discovery* with his report, Vancouver decided to personally make one last inspection of the area. As if to add witnesses to this important find, he asked Baker and Menzies to accompany him on what was planned as a four day tour. In addition to viewing the main thread of the inlet, they poked into every incoming stream and every indentation in the shore which might hold even the thinnest hope of providing a further extension of navigable waterway. During this tour they had another of a series of encounters with the native population, all reasonably friendly. When the inspection party returned to the *Discovery*, and astronomical observations were rechecked, Vancouver recorded the final termination and northern extent of Cook's Inlet to be latitude 61° 29' North, longitude 211° 17' East.

Returning south through Cook's Inlet the *Discovery* was finally rejoined with the *Chatham*. With the completion of some fill-in surveys around the entrance to that Inlet by May 15, they were ready to proceed east along the southerly shores of Alaska. Over the next three months this phase of the work would include Prince William Sound, site of one of the worst oil spills in the 20th century, and Cross Sound, west of Juneau, the present day capital of Alaska. During this period the ships and the long boat crews had numerous contacts with Russians and their fur trading stations. The Russians had been established in the area for about fifty years. They were generally friendly, but accomplishing any business with them was made very difficult by the lack of competent translators.

By mid-August the ships were once more at Port Conclusion, the location near Point Baker where the previous year's surveys had terminated. While preparations were made to sail south, Whidbey and Mr. Johnstone completed such surveys as were necessary to thoroughly tie the two year's work together. Vancouver was finally able to declare, "The principal object which His Majesty appears to have had in view, in directing the undertaking of this voyage having at length been completed, I trust the precision with which the survey of the coast of North West America has been carried into effect, will remove every doubt, and set aside every opinion of a north-west passage..".

It was time for an extra issue of grog for all hands—it was time to head for home.

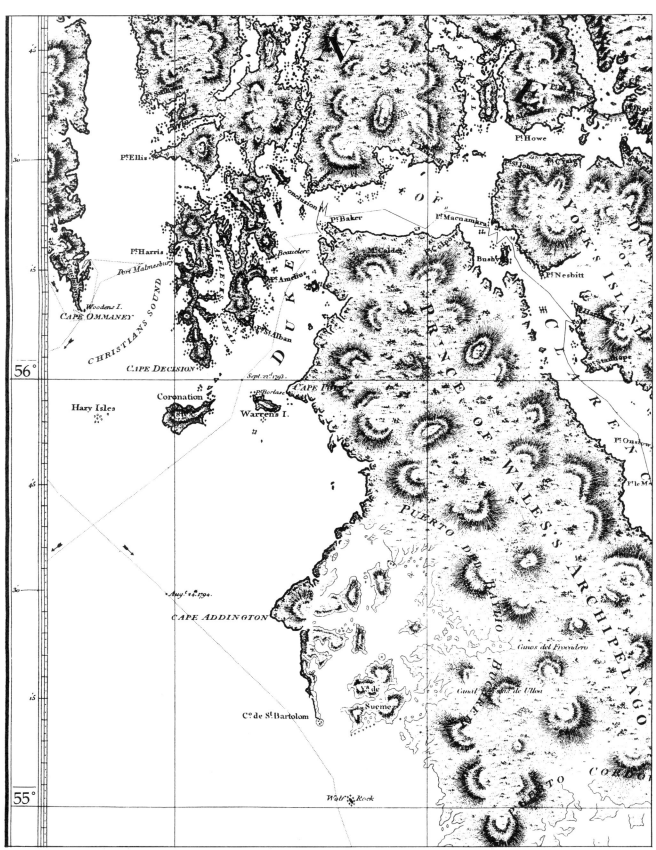

Portion of Plate 7 (See Appendix B)
Baker's chart showing Pt. Baker, and the vicinity where
the exploration was concluded.

CHAPTER 6

Homeward Bound—First Command

The homeward departure from Port Conclusion was delayed for several days by foul weather, a southeast gale with very heavy rain, thick fog—actually typical fall conditions for the Gulf of Alaska. The recognition that waiting for better weather was not a promising strategy, plus the boredom of inactivity motivated the August 22 departure. Rough seas and strong headwinds provided several days of most uncomfortable and very dangerous sailing as they worked the ships off the rocky Alaska coast to open water. At one point, the danger of being driven onto a lee shore was so great that the small boats were launched to provide a tow, during the course of which, crewman Isaac Wooden fell overboard and drowned. In commemoration of this well regarded, A.B. (able bodied) seaman from *Chatham*, Vancouver designated the large rock which lies off Cape Ommaney, Wooden's Rock.

As they continued southeast and south off the coastline, every opportunity was taken, weather permitting, to double check the charts they had previously prepared. These charts represented a major part of the expedition's accomplishments, certainly Baker's major contribution to the mission. Vancouver's professional standards would require every possible effort to assure their accuracy.

When they reached Friendly Cove on Nootka Sound on the evening of September 2, Vancouver found the news both sad and discouraging. First, he learned that his "highly valuable and much esteemed friend, Senior Quadra, had in the month of March died at St. Blas, universally lamented." During their yet uncompleted joint efforts to resolve their conflicting instructions as to the disposition of the Spanish holding at Nootka, they had developed a high respect and warm personal regard for each other. Quadra had been replaced by Brigadier General Don Jose Manuel Alava as the Spanish Governor of Nootka. The second piece of bad news was that no clarification of instructions on resolving the Nootka matter had been received through Lt. Broughton or any other courier from England, or by Gen. Alava through Spanish channels. The frustration of this situation was exceeded only by the alarm

Vancouver and his officers felt upon hearing from English fur-trading captains in the harbor at Nootka, recently arrived from the Orient, as to the deteriorating state of Europe due to the French revolution.

Vancouver resolved to remain at Nootka until mid-October, with the hope that some ship would arrive with the long awaited new instructions which could enable him and Gen. Alava to conclude the Nootka disposition matter, the last piece of unfinished business of the expedition. Meantime the officers and crew were kept busy making much needed repairs to the ships in preparation for the long trip home. The spirit of civility between English and Spanish crews, established on earlier visits when Quadra was in command, was continued by Gen. Alava. Scarce materials and skilled craftsmen were generously shared. The officers reciprocated in hosting shipboard dinners.

With the approach of mid-October, the prospect of increasingly stormy seas, and the lack of any further word from England, Vancouver resolved to make a final departure from Nootka. With the minimum required repairs complete, the *Discovery* and *Chatham* put to sea on October 17, bound for Monterey. General Alava was to leave the following day aboard the *Princessa* with the same destination.

The *Discovery* arrived at Monterey on November 6, preceded by the *Chatham*. Vancouver was again disappointed to learn that there were no dispatches from England for him. Senior Arguello, the lieutenant of the Presidio at Monterey, acting in the absence of the Governor, understood Vancouver's desire to resolve if at all possible, the Nootka matter. He ordered a special courier to go to San Diego to ascertain whether the most recent ship arriving from Spain might have brought any dispatch for Vancouver. During the ten days required for the courier to return, the crews replenished their water supply, and enjoyed the first opportunity in months to have an unlimited supply of fresh food, and to dry out completely.

During this same interval, a dispatch for Gen. Alava did arrive from the Spanish Viceroy in Mexico. It relayed information from Spain, confirming that Lt.

Broughton had safely returned to Europe with the reports and recommendations from Vancouver. It indicated that another mission was being prepared in London to follow up on the Nootka matter, and that pending the arrival of this mission, no further action should be taken on that issue. It is important to note that this was information from Spain, not from London, and not directed to Vancouver. In fact, it later proved to be true, but for the moment it did not alter the reasons supporting Vancouver's decision to head for home—a major portion of the overall mission accomplished, a weary crew and ships even more weary. The final straw was provided when the courier returned from San Diego empty-handed.

Since any chance of Lt. Broughton returning to resume his position in the expedition could now be dismissed, Vancouver decided to make permanent several reassignments in his command. These included designating Lt. Joseph Baker as first lieutenant on the *Discovery*, Lt. Peter Puget as captain of the *Chatham*.[1]

During the three weeks they had spent at Monterey, Baker had completed another remarkable task. At Vancouver's request, he prepared duplicate copies of all of the principal charts covering their survey of the North American coast. One copy was sent by dispatch to the Spanish Viceroy of Mexico, to be relayed on to England. This was a hedge against the possibility that a disaster at sea on the way home would wipe out the product of three year's work. The second copy was given to Gen. Alava in fulfilment of a commitment Vancouver had made to Quadra three years earlier. The set of charts Baker had prepared numbered eight, and included coverage of all the areas stipulated in the expedition's orders. A catalog of these charts is included in Appendix B.

One final piece of business with the Spanish remained—the return of three British deserters which they held captive. One in particular, a marine from the original *Chatham* crew, could expect a generous helping of the lash and a lonely trip home.

Vancouver's Journal, meticulously kept with almost daily entrees, begins at this point to include an increasing number of references to the "very debilitated state of my health." It was a good-days/bad-days sort of thing, which he seemed able to rise above when a particular event fired his energies. And though the condition did not shake his confidence in maintaining command, it clearly preyed on his mind and must have added a measure of difficulty to the task of his first Lt. Joseph Baker.

Discovery and *Chatham* departed Monterey on December 2, 1794, amply resupplied even if not totally ship-shape. The planned course contemplated three near term checkpoints. The first was Cabo San Lucas at the southern tip of Baja California. This present day popular resort area was, in the late 1700s, of note only as a location for which the latitude and longitude had been well established. It provided Vancouver and Baker another opportunity to check their own calculations, and with which they were well satisfied. It also provided a chance to check the accuracy of the several chronometers the expedition was using to test a new and hopefully simplified method of determining longitude. Of the four instruments they had, Arnold's No. 14 was found to be the most accurate.[2]

The second checkpoint was the Island of Cocos, at present day a possession of Costa Rica, and located approximately 300 miles southwest thereof. This island was of importance to mariners of the day for its generous supply of fresh water. The water and the warm climate had induced at least one earlier mariner to plant vegetables and leave pigs to multiply, measures taken on several of the far flung Pacific islands to provide emergency supplies. Unfortunately the precise location of Cocos had been variously and erroneously reported, a fact Vancouver meant to correct. The island was located on January 20. During the next eight days it was inspected by shore parties under the direction of Whidbey. Precise and exhaustive observations were made to establish the location as Lat. 5° 35'12" North, and Long. 273° 05'26" East. Once again the combination of Whidbey's field notes and Baker's engineering added another chart to the folio which accompanies Vancouver's Journal. On January 28, 1795 the expedition departed Cocos with the intention of proceeding to the Island of Juan Fernandez, west of Chile, but on a course which would take them close to the Galapagos Islands. This group of islands, lying on the equator approximately 600 miles west of Equador, had been visited by numerous mariners and with varying reports as to their precise location. Vancouver had no intention of further delaying the passage home for a complete inspection. He did hope to further the application of his professional navigator's skills by verifying the precise location. From February 2 to February 11 they cruised slowly along the westerly side of the island group. Whidbey and Menzies made a brief shore visit on the largest island, Albemarle, and reported the rather barren volcanic nature of the terrain. Ship's crew found the fishing to be some of the best they had seen. Baker added a chart of a portion of the Island of Albemarle to the folio. Vancouver noted that he "...continued to labour under a very indifferent state of health."

The next designated rendezvous was to be the island of Juan Fernandez, off the coast of Chile, where they planned to make final preparations for the treacherous passage around Cape Horn. Juan Fernandez Island was reportedly the setting for Daniel Defoe's famous novel, "Robinson Crusoe," written in about 1720. Enroute to this waypoint, *Chatham* became separated from *Discovery* for a time, during which Puget had a chance meeting with a Spanish merchant vessel. The captain informed Puget that no facilities or assistance for making ship repairs were to be found on that island, and recommended the mainland port of Valpariso, Chile.

Meantime, *Discovery* had been caught in a sudden gale and suffered extensive damage to her sails, and to her main topgallant mast. Slowed considerably, it wasn't long before the *Chatham* was sighted climbing up over the horizon from astern. After receiving Puget's report, and considering the poor condition of the *Discovery*, Vancouver was forced, reluctantly, to consider changing course for Valpariso. His reluctance stemmed from the fact that his orders directed him to avoid Spanish ports north of latitude 30° south, and Valpariso was well within the forbidden area. The orders allowed an exception for emergencies, and Vancouver got Puget, Baker, and Whidbey to sign a memorandum expressing agreement that an emergency did indeed exist. This unusual procedure suggests a deterioration in Vancouver's command confidence, paralleling his increasing notations of failing health.

On anchoring at Valpariso, March 25, the reception from local authorities was so favorable as to put aside any apprehensions they might have had about entering this port. Colonel Alava, the officer in charge, proved to be the brother of the officer at Monterey with whom Vancouver had had good relations. After arranging for space and assistance in making repairs to the ships, Vancouver procured an apartment ashore under conditions he felt would favor his health.

As the work on the ships progressed, the officers and crew were shown the warmest of hospitality in the homes and activities of this closeknit community. The President of Chile in Santiago, a three day horesback ride from Valpariso, extended a cordial invitation for Vancouver and his officers to visit the capital. His deteriorating health notwithstanding, this invitation was treated by Vancouver as a command appearance. The president sent two officer escorts, who turned out to be natives of Ireland. They assisted in procuring a sufficient number of saddle horses and pack mules, at twelve (Spanish) dollars each for the round trip.

His Excellency Don Ambrosio Higgins de Vallenar, President of Chile, personally greeted his guests with a warmth and graciousness which overcame any of the pain understandably experienced by a group of career sailors after a three day horseback ride. They were surprised to be greeted in fluent English until they learn'd that His Excellency was a native of Ireland. At an early period in his life he had entered the army of England, but later found greater opportunities for advancement in the army of Spain. He was most interested in getting a firsthand account of Vancouver's voyage of exploration, and he expressed pleasure in the opportunity to converse in his native tongue.[3]

Several days of touring the city, introductions to

73

Valparaiso, Chile, as sketched by Midshipman Sykes.

Vancouver's Journal

prominent citizens, and entertainment ensued. The highlight was certainly the banquet hosted by Senior Cotappas, a wealthy Spanish merchant. A portion of Vancouver's description certainly portrays a sharp break from the rigors of sea life:

"We should have been extremely happy to have availed ourselves of the pressing entreaties of Senior Catappas to join with the ladies in dancing, but as their country dances appeared to be very difficult, and as no one amongst us could recollect the figures of any of those we had been accustomed to in England, we were under the mortification of acknowledging our ignorance, and declining the intended civility of the master of the house. From this disappointment in the pleasures of the evening we were, however, in some measure relieved, by some of the ladies, who had retired from the dance, sending us a message, requesting we would join their party on the cushions; with this we instantly complied, and considered ourselves greatly indebted for this mark of condescension, as it was departing from the established rules of their society on such occasions. The generalty of the ladies in Santiago are not wanting in personal charms, and most of those we had the pleasure of meeting this evening might rather be considered handsome....but in the total neglect of their teeth...".

George Vancouver was ever the perfectionist—on land or sea.

Meanwhile back in Valpariso, repairs to the ships were not proceeding as anticipated. The removal of each yardarm or mast seemed to reveal more wear, tear and rot. From the time the officers returned from Santiago, hoping to depart promptly, it took another ten days of effort to put the ships in a minimum state of readiness for the voyage ahead. The delay of each day in departing was a matter of increasing concern. In the southern hemisphere, winter was approaching and with it, the increasing chance of violent storms off Cape Horn. On May 6, after firing the appropriate thirteen gun salute, *Discovery* and *Chatham* sailed out of Valpariso. The next appointed rendezvous was St. Helena, the British island navy base in the south Atlantic Ocean, some 8,000 miles away.

For the first ten days the weather remained tolerable, but the mountainous swells reflected the unimpeded sweep of the prevailing winds across 7,000 miles of the south Pacific Ocean. As they continued south, the winds increased to gale strength, with much heavier gusts. Just as a set of the sails would be completed, a violent squall would strike, rending sails like the tired old rags they had become. Braces and sheets parted and anchor lines had to be substituted. No sooner were sails reefed then they had to be struck. Finally topgallant yardarms and topgallant masts had to be lowered to the deck to relieve the stress on the principal masts. Canvas was reduced to courses (lowest sails) and even to storm staysails.

By May 26, as they approached the latitude of Cape Horn, the heavy rain squalls turned to hail, and then to snow. Keeping *Chatham* in sight became difficult, then impossible. Even more critical was the reduced visibility for taking sun shots to determine latitude. Sextants were kept at the ready to snatch any opportunity to gauge the altitude of the sun, which would tell them when it was safe to change course to the east and be certain to avoid the rocks and islands off the tip of Terra del Fuego. All hands not too sick to stand, or too frozen to grab a line, were kept busy relashing anything loose or manning the pumps to stem the water coming in through leaks in the *Discovery's* bow. Whenever Vancouver sighted *Chatham*, he would signal, urging the bending on of more sail so that the slower moving ship could stay in company. Only later would Vancouver learn from Puget that at times, the smaller *Chatham* had been so tossed about that he had only five men still on their feet, and that they had been "..comparatively speaking, almost under water during the greater part of the passage."

At last, on May 28, they reached the approximate latitude of south 57° and were able to "fetch the Horn." A change of course to the northeast brought some relief in the weather, but only on a relative scale. In fact, during another of the recurring storms, midway between Cape Horn and St. Helena, the

Discovery suffered its final crew casualty, when seaman Richard Jones fell overboard from the main mast ratlines and was drowned.

Early in the afternoon of July 2, 1795, the foretop lookout signalled the sighting of St. Helena Island. As they reduced sail to approach the anchorage, they observed a sizable formation of ships apparently departing to the north in convoy. Vancouver reported in to the Governor, who confirmed the matter of the observed convoy, and provided a quick update on the status of war with France.

The strategic mission of Vancouver's expedition was now complete. There remained several administrative matters to be accomplished, and the overwhelming desire of all hands to get home. Immediate steps were taken to make minimal repairs and to reprovision the ships' stores, now well depleted after the 58 day passage from Valpariso. Ships' calendars were set back one day to correct for the day gained on their easterly circumnavigation (Chapter 1). Per Vancouver's orders, all personal logs, journals, and charts were collected from the officers and crew, for delivery to the Admiralty.

The need to deliver important dispatches to a British army in Brazil, resulted in orders for Puget to sail *Chatham* for the port of St. Salvador enroute to England. Vancouver and Baker departed St. Helena as soon as possible, hoping to catch up to the slow moving convoy, thus gaining protection from French raiders. They joined the convoy on August 21, and were made welcome by the commander, Captain Essington. Troubled by the vulnerability of his collection of transports to a heavily gunned enemy squadron, Essington had decided to stay well to the west of France, and to put into the estuary of the River Shannon, on the west side of Ireland, there to await heavier naval protection.

The convoy put into Shannon on September 13, with Vancouver in a fit of anxiety to deliver his report to the Admiralty. He sought and received orders to leave the *Discovery* and proceed by whatever means, overland and across the Irish Sea, to London. Vancouver bade a heartfelt farewell to his crew and "..to my first lieutenant Mr. Baker, in whose zeal for the service, and abilities as an officer, a long experience justified me in implicitly confiding; I resigned my command of the *Discovery* into his hands...".

Thirty eight days later Baker worked *Discovery* into dock in the Thames River—the end of the expedition. *Discovery* was a seriously weakened ship. Her planks and decks were leaking, her masts were sprung, and her sails were in tatters. But to Lieutenant Joseph Baker of His Majesty's Navy, she was nearly the most beautiful thing a young officer could see—his first command.

CHAPTER 7

The Vashon Connection

The Joseph Baker who returned in October 1795, was a very different man from the young, freshly minted third Lieutenant who had departed England nearly five years earlier. From the lowliest officer aboard Vancouver's ship *Discovery*, he had proven his worth as a valued member of the Captain's staff. He had earned his progress to the rank of first Lieutenant and had tasted the responsibilities of command. The maturing qualities of these experiences must have given him a sense of confidence in himself, in his career, and in his readiness to enjoy the social scene at home in England.

Baker lost little time in making contact with his mentor, Captain James Vashon. The most likely setting for that reunion would have been the west midlands town of Ludlow, Shropshire. It was in this ancient and still picturesque town that Vashon had been born and educated, and to which he returned throughout his life whenever his active naval career permitted. Several sources report his birthdate to be August 9, 1742, the second son of Rev. James Volant Vashon. His father was the Vicar at the church in the village of Eye, some seven miles to the south. James Vashon (the family pronounces the name, Vash'n) entered the navy in August 1755, at the age of thirteen, aboard *HMS Revenge* (Captain Cornwall), 28 guns. His early years as a midshipman included assignments to several ships, large and small, and he saw combat duty in the Mediterranean Sea, the coast of North America and the Caribbean.

Ludlow castle, center of official and festive activities since the 12th century.

Vashon passed the examination signalling completion of Midshipman training on September 7, 1763. Unfortunately, he had lost the patronage of two senior officers who could have been expected to recommend his promotion. Rear-Admiral Charles Holmes, who had expressed some concern about Vashon's boyish appearance, died in November 1761, and Captain Goostrey, in command of the *Cambridge* on which Vashon was currently assigned, was killed in July 1762, in the attack on Morro Castle, Havana. Vashon continued as a Midshipman in very active service in the Caribbean and off Newfoundland until 1772. By then the major navy cutback which followed the end of England's Seven Years War with France and Spain, reached the *Quebec*, Vashon's current ship on West Indies Station. Two thirds of the fleet was called back to England, paid off and laid up in ordinary. Vashon, like most of his fellow officers, was removed from active duty, left to exist on scanty half pay. Crews were simply turned loose with nothing more than whatever small sum might remain due in their pay account.

By 1774, England was again mobilizing its fleet in response to the deteriorating relations with the American colonies. The dreaded pressgangs were again turned loose along waterfront communities to "recruit" hands for the King's expanded navy. The recall of officers brought Vashon back from two years of forced vacation at Ludlow. He somehow came to the attention of Admiral Sir George Rodney, who made him a Lieutenant of the frigate *Maidstone*, again assigned to the West Indies. So far, Vashon's career progress had been unusually slow—Lieutenant at age 32 was indeed rare—but that was about to change!

First assigned as 2nd Lieutenant on the *Maidstone*, Vashon was shortly promoted to 1st Lieutenant, as the result of the promotion and transfer of Lieutenant (later Admiral) Peter Rainier, a name destined for prominence in Washington State geography. Still aboard the *Maidstone* in 1779, he participated in the capture of the French ship *Lion* off the coast of Delaware. Vashon was put aboard the badly damaged *Lion*, in charge of a twenty-four man prize

crew and 200 prisoners (!) with orders to try to reach the major British naval base at Antigua. The difficult salvage mission was accomplished, and Vashon was rewarded with an immediate promotion to the rank of Commander, with orders to return to England. Upon return to Ludlow, he was further rewarded with the hand in marriage of Jane Bethell, a marriage unfortunately not to be blessed with long life.

The rank of Commander required something to command, and for Vashon the orders assigned him to the *Alert*, listed as a brig-sloop, with a length of 78 feet, a beam of 25 feet and carrying 14 guns. After an initial period on patrol in the North Sea, *Alert* was ordered to the Caribbean for convoy and patrol duty with the two squadrons commanded by Admiral Sir George Rodney and Admiral Sir Hyde Parker. Toward the end of 1780, Vashon was ordered back to England where the *Alert* was involved in further North Sea patrol duty, again under the command of Admiral Hyde Parker. These patrols were of relatively short duration, affording Vashon more frequent opportunities to return to Ludlow to visit his wife and family. However, it is apparent that Admiral Parker was not his favorite commanding officer, and by late 1781, he obtained reassignment to Admiral Rodney's squadron in the Caribbean.

Before departing England, *Alert* was briefly laid up for repairs, giving Vashon time for one more visit to Ludlow. It was at this time that young Joseph Baker launched his naval career by signing on to be Commander Vashon's cabin boy, (see Chapter 2). Whether there was a prior close family relationship between the Bakers and the Vashons is not clear from any available record. An arrangement such as Joseph's enlistment usually involved special consideration, such as close friendships, family ties, and in some cases, money. The fact that Joseph Baker's mother's maiden name was Ludlow, suggests numerous possible bases for the enlistment arrangements. Whatever the motivations were, the clear and happy fact is that this was the beginning of a warm friendship based on deep mutual respect, destined to last throughout the lives of both men.

The experiences shared by Vashon and Baker during the 1782-84 period, (described in Chapter 2) provided the defining events for Baker's future career. they included service aboard both mammoth ships-of-the-line, such as *Prince William* and *Formidable*, with crews numbering in the hundreds and the accompanying formal, impersonal atmosphere, and the much smaller sloops and frigates such as *Alert* and *Sybil*, demanding much more advanced sailing skills, and a well drilled team of crew members to get performance. In the early years of Vashon's career he seemed to prefer the smaller ship commands, a frequent choice of aggressive commanders who enjoyed the challenge of the relatively greater speed and maneuverability of the

*Captain (later Admiral) James Vashon, Baker's
first Captain and career-long mentor.*

sloop and the smaller frigates. These were typically three-masted vessels in the range of 100 to 150 feet in length, and carrying from 20 to 50 guns. They were assigned the duty of convoy protection, where their maneuverability was essential to fend off attacks, or to "cutting out" missions, where the opportunities to capture enemy vessels and win prize money were far greater than for the crews on the large ships-of-the-line. Baker also acquired the taste and the talent for the smaller fighting ship, and was favored with that type of assignment in most of his later commands.

By 1783, following the conclusion of the American revolution, England was again scaling back its navy. Vashon was ordered to bring his ship *Sybil* back from the Caribbean to be paid off. There followed two years of inactive duty at half pay, and another opportunity to return to Ludlow.

His career which had been slow to develop, now seemed well established—but half pay was no confidence builder. His two widowed sisters were living together in the village of Presteigne, Wales, just 15 miles to the southwest of Ludlow. The younger of the two, Mrs. Elizabeth Weyermann, had a daughter, now ten, also named Elizabeth, who was the "apple of his eye." Her father had died when she was very young, and Vashon had become as much substitute father as uncle. As to his own family, the story turns sad indeed. His wife gave birth to a son, James Volant Vashon in 1784, but, perhaps due to attendant complications, she died in 1786. The outlook for a career naval officer with a motherless child must have been bleak indeed. Fortunately for all, Vashon found and married a new wife, and who should it be, but Sarah Rainier, a younger sister of his earlier shipmate, now Captain (later Admiral) Peter Rainier.

Vashon was recalled to active duty late in 1786. His assignment, *HMS Europa*, 50 guns, with a promotion to Captain. *Europa* was at the time serving as the flagship for Commodore Alan Gardner, Commander-in-Chief of the Jamaica squadron. He had formed a favorable impression of Vashon in earlier commands and accordingly requested his services as flag

Captain. In turn, Vashon requested Baker as one of his Midshipmen, and Baker joined the *Europa* in Jamaica on December 9, 1786. The officer list of the *Europa* included Lieutenant George Vancouver, and another Midshipman by the name of Peter Puget (see Chapter 2).

Commodore Gardner and his wife, Susan, were people of considerable means and influence. When, in 1789 the Admiralty was planning another mission of exploration to the South Seas, he was effective in recommending that Vancouver be named second in command, under Captain Roberts (see Chapter 3). Vashon was subsequently transferred to command of the battleship *Ardent* (64 guns), later to the *St. Albans*, and finally, in 1794, to the even larger battleship *Pompee* (80 guns). After the resumption of war with France in 1793, his assigned areas of operation shifted to blockade duty along the French coast.

Vashon was thus engaged when he received word, in 1795, of the return of the Vancouver expedition, and he no doubt swelled with pride to learn that his protege, Joseph Baker, had arrived with the rank of 1st Lieutenant of the flagship, *Discovery*, and in command of that ship for the last leg of the voyage.

For Joseph Baker a homecoming celebration was certainly in order, but where, and with whom? His parents and most of his siblings were dead; his oldest brother had emigrated to America. The person he surely wanted most to regale with the story of his recent adventures was his mentor, Captain James Vashon. And that being the case, the location would be Ludlow.

The architectural and commercial axis of 18th century Ludlow was defined by two major structures, the ancient castle and the beautiful St. Laurence's Parish Church. Construction of the castle was commenced near the close of the eleventh century, as part of the defense system against the guerrilla raids by the yet unconquered Welsh. It is situated on a well defendable position overlooking the River Teme. The homes and shops of suppliers of services to the castle clustered outside the wall in a village first named Dinham. As the village grew to a town the name was changed to "Lodelowe," (meaning "hill by the rapids or loud

Captain (later Admiral) Peter Rainier, brother of Vashon's wife.

waters"), and much later to Ludlow. St. Laurence's, located about a quarter-mile east of the castle, rests on a 12th century foundation, but was mostly rebuilt between 1433 and 1471. The hexagonal south porch is early 14th century design and reflects Ludlow's close commercial links with the port city of Bristol, where there is a similar design feature at St. Mary's Redcliffe. During the 16th and 17th centuries the castle became the headquarters of the Council of Marches of Wales. This administrative center attracted judges, lawyers and civil servants to the town, which was described at that time as a "bureaucratic anthill." Also, many of the landed gentry from the surrounding estates built townhouses in Ludlow so they could enjoy the rich cultural and social activities, supported by the flourishing export trade in wool and manufactured cloth.

By 1795, the pace of commercial and social activity was approaching a zenith, though such events are only apparent in retrospect. To the wool trade had been added outstanding success in the manufacture of gloves. The cultural attractions now included two theatres and numerous festivals. Stylish promenades around the castle grounds were popular, and for the sporting set there was a nearby horse racing course. One of the centers of festive activity then, and today a symbol of historic England was The Feathers (Inn), described more recently as "an architectural wonder, beamed and braced, leaning and sometimes seeming to totter." Ludlow historian, David Lloyd, in his book, "Country Grammar School,"[1] quotes the wife of an early nineteenth century parson who, in writing about her Ludlow girlhood, seems to best capture the flavor of this period: "Mary Sneade loved to tell her own daughters of the pure fun and frivolity of her first Ludlow season ...Broad Street gay with rapid feet and glancing eyes, the shopping expeditions for to-morrow's ball; the little encounters with partners from last night's ball; scarlet coats and blue and black...".

It would have been late in the fall of 1795 by the time Joseph Baker could have arrived in Ludlow. In the early winter weather and the shortened days, Broad Street would have been less gay, and the promenades around the castle would surely have been over for the season. But for Joseph Baker it was not the social whirl that caught his fancy. For him, the high point of the year, save for return from the arduous expedition was the chance to become acquainted (or reacquainted) with Vashon's niece, Elizabeth Weyermann. The record is not clear as to how well, if at all, Joseph and Elizabeth were acquainted prior to the departure of the Vancouver Expedition in the Spring of 1791. In either event, she would then have been but a teenage girl, and he a twenty-three year old junior Lieutenant of tentative prospects, hardly ready for serious commitment. How very different was the scene now at the end of 1795. Elizabeth was a young lady of twenty-one. Joseph had the maturing experience of worldwide travel.

They shared many elements of cultural background. They also shared the warm approbation of "Uncle Jim" Vashon, who promptly re-extended his protective hand by making Joseph 1st Lieutenant of his current command, ship-of-the-line, *Pompee*. The *Pompee* was on blockade duty with the Channel Fleet, which made it less difficult for Joseph to visit Elizabeth with reasonable frequency. The relationship ripened during 1796 and blossomed to marriage early in 1797. At approximately the same time, his shipmate, Peter Puget was marrying Hannah Elrington.

Joseph and Elizabeth Baker established their home in Presteigne, Wales, a short distance from

The Feathers Inn, Ludlow.

Leith Harbor, 1992. Note the manual capstan of the type used to position and careen ships at the time Baker and Vashon served here.

Ludlow, no doubt so she could have the company of her mother and her aunt during those many periods between the departures and the homecomings that were the life of a naval officer. Those periods were not so many or of such duration but what over the twenty years of their marriage, they would have ten children, seven sons and three daughters.

HMS Pompee would be the last ship on which Baker and Vashon would serve simultaneously. On March 1, 1799, Baker was promoted to the rank of Commander, and shortly given command of the brig *Calypso* (16 guns, 102x28). His three years aboard *Calypso* included some brisk action in the Caribbean, and convoy duty in the North Sea. April 26, 1802, brought Baker the much coveted promotion to Captain. That date would establish the order of all further promotions, whether on active duty, half-pay inactive duty, and even beyond retirement. He was also given command of the frigate *Castor* (32 guns, 126x35), with mainly convoy duty in the North Sea and the Baltic Sea.

On April 23, 1804, James Vashon was promoted to the rank of Rear-Admiral and assigned command of the naval squadron operating out of the Port of Leith, on the southerly shore of the Firth of Forth. A separate seaport town at the time, Leith has since become a part of metropolitan Edinburgh, Capital of Scotland.

Leith had been an important port for several centuries, serving as a focal point in the brisk trade between Scotland and the ports of southeast England, and extending to the northern European countries of Sweden, Denmark, Northern Germany, Holland, Belgium and France. For the previous two hundred years the principal exports had been linen, woollen goods, hides, oats, fish, salt, coal and livestock. Returning ships brought flax, timber, wines, silks and other fine materials. By the end of the eighteenth century, Scotland was taking a leading position in the industrial revolution. The focus of imports was shifting to raw materials, and exports increasingly consisted of manufactured goods, high value cargoes, the basis for Scotland's growing prosperity. These cargoes attracted attention well beyond the realm of normal commerce,

namely from the navies of one or another of the countries with which England repeatedly found itself at war, or the privateers and pirates to be encountered at any time, war or no war. This scourge of the export trade was not confined to just local adversaries either. Quick sailing American privateers did much damage along Scotland's east coast during the 1770s. Indeed, the "Father of the American Navy," John Paul Jones (who was born in Scotland) sent the panicky Edinburgh Town Council scurrying to the Admiralty for protection, when in 1779, in his flagship *Bonhomme Richard*, he led a squadron into the harbor at Leith. And it was only a few miles south of Leith that, in the course of a desperate battle with *HMS Serapis*, Jones uttered his famous rallying cry, "I have not yet begun to fight."

The merchants had tried a number of schemes to combat these depredations to trade, with only limited success. One of the better tactics was to assemble groups of departing merchant ships under the protection of a few hired gun-ships. By 1804, when Vashon was ordered to Leith, the problem had grown to a matter of national concern, well beyond the capacity of the merchants' self-help resources. To the long standing problem of marauding privateers, there was an increasing threat from France, later formalized as Napoleon's "continental system," his strategy of using his formidable navy to eliminate British trade from all of Europe.

By 1805 Admiral Vashon had instituted a formal convoy system, and on March 27, from his flagship *HMS Roebuck* in Leith roads, he sent the following report to the Lord Provost:

"The departure of the convoys last season was regulated as nearly as possible to the times of the new and full moons at which periods the vessels could always get out of the harbour and immediately after the departure of one convoy advice was sent to the Lord Provost of the time fixed for the next to sail. This is the plan I propose to pursue as far as I am able during the present season, and I have to request your Lordship will be pleased to impress on the minds of the merchants and ship owners the necessity of having their ships ready by the days appointed."[2]

Ludlow 1992. Note entrance through ancient town wall.
Vashon's retirement house at extreme left of photograph.

Plain enough. The reference to "new and full moons" related to the fact that these would be times of highest flood tide, thus assuring maximum maneuvering room in clearing harbors. The convoy system instituted by Vashon was evidently a resounding success, as the record indicates that during the ensuing five years, only two privateer attacks on ships departing Leith resulted in losses.

While at Leith, Vashon was promoted to Vice-Admiral in 1808. Finally, toward the end of that year, Vashon determined it was time to "strike his flag" and retire. So pleased were the merchants of Leith with the protection he had given their commerce that they gave him a public dinner, at which he was awarded two commemorative plates and the honorary designation of Freeman of the City of Edinburgh. At a somewhat similar event in Ludlow, several years earlier, at which Admiral Lord Nelson was named Freeman of Ludlow, Nelson said of Vashon:

"As to myself I have done no more than my duty, no more than others would have done in the same situation, and there is one present (looking at then Captain Vashon) whom I am happy to call my friend, whom I feel convinced from my own knowledge of his character and long acquaintance with him, only wants the opportunity to prove himself equally deserving of the approbation of his fellow townsmen and the gratitude of his country."

Such was the warm regard in which Vashon was held at the conclusion of his naval career. He had served on the active list for 54 years, a remarkable record for that, or any, age. He and his wife, Sarah would be favored with nineteen years of happy retirement, during which he would receive promotion to Admiral in 1821. Life in Ludlow, at No 54 Broad Street where he retired was sweeter than ever. The house remains today, and is marked with a Ludlow Civic Society plaque.

Admiral James Vashon died in 1827 and was interred at St. Laurence's Parish Church in Ludlow. The inscription on the memorial plaque reads: "Sacred to the Memory of James Vashon Esq. Admiral of the White who died Oct. 20, 1827 aged 85." Adjacent plaques read: "Also Jane, his wife who died Dec. 4, 1785 aged 42 years; and Also Sarah, his wife who died March 2, 1832 aged 82."

CHAPTER 8

The Years Beyond—Ecstasy & Agony

Joseph and Elizabeth Baker established their home on St. David Street in Presteigne, Wales, early in 1797. It remained their home base throughout the twenty years of their marriage. Her mother and her mother's sister, both widows, also lived on St. David Street. They were thus able to provide companionship for Elizabeth when Joseph was away at sea, and grandmotherly assistance when needed, and that would not be long. The first child, significantly named James Vashon Baker, arrived in 1798. The second, Elizabeth Grace, was born in 1800 but unfortunately died in infancy.

The year 1801 was marked by a joyous event when Joseph's old friend and shipmate, now Captain, Peter Puget and his wife Hannah, responding to the Baker's invitation, moved to Presteigne. The Pugets had decided that rented apartment living in the urban atmosphere of London, was no place to raise a family. With their four young sons, they first settled into a country house on the outskirts of Presteigne, and later moved to the more prestigious "Red House" fronting on Broad Street.[1] That home is still providing a pleasant living situation in 1992. That the two families enjoyed each others' company is evidenced by the fact that, in 1803, the Pugets named their fifth child, Joseph Baker Puget. The Bakers responded by naming their fourth child, Josephine Puget Baker, and their fifth child, Peter Puget Baker.

After Joseph Baker was promoted to the rank of Captain, in 1802 and given command of the frigate, *Castor* (32 guns, 126x35) his base of operations was at Leith, Scotland. On occasions when the ship was to be laid up for repairs, Elizabeth would join him at Leith in temporary quarters. From 1804 to 1808, when "Uncle Jim Vashon" was the Admiral in command of the base, this was no doubt a very pleasant break from the more limited life in Presteigne, and certainly a pleasant break for Joseph from the miseries of North Sea patrols. It was just such a time in 1808, when Elizabeth gave birth to their sixth child, William Erskine Baker, destined for future fame as an Army General in India.

On May 10, 1808, the frigate *Tartar* departed Leith in pursuit of a Dutch raider, thought to be headed for the coast of Norway. On the 15th, attempting to sneak into the harbor at Bergen under Dutch colors, *Tartar* was attacked by a flotilla of small gunboats put out from shore. While Captain Bettesworth was attempting to aim one of his guns, a cannon ball from the gunboats removed his head. First Lieutenant Sykes managed to disengage, and on the 20th, brought the ship back to Leith. Captain Joseph Baker was reassigned to command the *Tartar*. And before he was through with her, he might well conclude that she was a jinxed ship. HMS *Tartar* was a frigate, a three masted fighting ship, carrying 32 guns, 26 twelve pounders and 6 six pounders. Launched in 1801, she was of the latest design of vessels which formed the attack arm of the navy. Fast and maneuverable, she was ideally suited for either blockade patrol or cutting out missions to capture enemy merchant ships. It was just the type of vessel that Baker preferred, and that he had shown aptitude in handling.

The more difficult task was keeping track of who the enemy was. The last decade of the 18th century and the first two decades of the 19th, brought a stream of political and military alignments and realignments among the nations surrounding the Baltic Sea. Sweden, Russia, Poland, Prussia, Pomerania (then controlled by Sweden, now part of Germany) and Denmark were to be found in various combinations, shifting almost yearly, from policies of neutrality or support with respect to either England or France. Currently, the deciding factor was most often the amount of intimidation being exerted by Napoleon. The one nearly constant, was a state of war between England and France. By 1806, Napoleon was endeavoring to impose his "continental system" on trade within the European community, which meant simply, freeze out England. England was attempting to maintain its important trade relations in the Baltic area, while blockading French ports from receiving strategic supplies.

At the time Baker took command of the *Tartar*, Sweden was promoting good relations with England. Notwithstanding long, close relations with France, Sweden was increasingly apprehensive about Napoleon's intentions, plus she hoped for England's

*Presteigne, Wales. The Puget family lived in the large brick
house on the left from 1801-1818. The Baker family lived
one block away.*

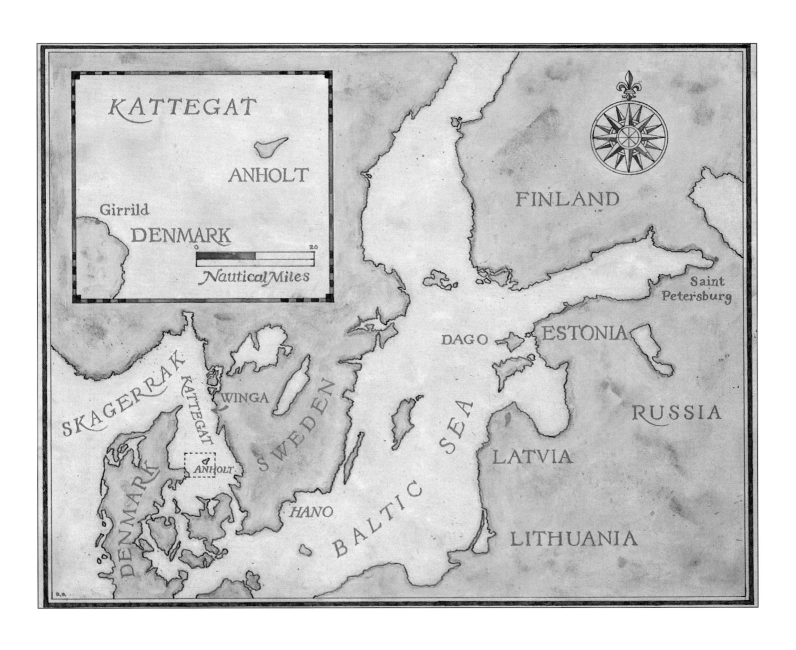

KATTEGAT

ANHOLT

Girrild

DENMARK

0   20

Nautical Miles

FINLAND

Saint
Petersburg

DAGO

ESTONIA

RUSSIA

SKAGERRAK

KATTEGAT

WINGA

S W E D E N

DENMARK

ANHOLT

HANO

LATVIA

B A L T I C   S E A

LITHUANIA

support in her plans to acquire Norway. Norway was then part of Denmark, which in turn, was firmly under the thumb of Napoleon. Sweden provided England continuing access to the ports of Pomerania, plus permission to maintain a Baltic Sea naval command headquarters at Winga Sound, just outside the Swedish port city of Gothenburg. Thus Baker operated *Tartar* out of the naval base at Leith, Scotland, but as part of the Baltic fleet under the command of Vice Admiral Sir James Saumarez, at Winga Sound.

Baker's missions were typically patrols of several months duration, ranging through the Skagerrak, the Kattegat, through the Helsingborg Channel into the Baltic Sea as far as the Gulf of Finland and the then Russian Capital of St. Petersburg. The Baltic could produce extremely rough seas, and in the winter, bitter cold winds with ice in some harbors. The tasks included convoying transports, blockading unfriendly ports, and capturing foreign trading vessels and privateers preying on friendly vessels. The duty varied from deadly boring to just plain deadly with frequent hit-and-run combat. A patrol was usually performed by at least two frigates, and by 1810, Baker was typically the senior captain in charge of the patrol.

A break in this routine with an opportunity to return home in Presteigne, would ordinarily be Baker's fondest dream. However, just such an occasion in January , 1811, was tempered with a note of sadness. On January 6, he addressed a letter to his superiors, stating "..that having received sudden information of the death of a very near relative, my presence is urgently required with my family...". The letter included assurances that since *Tartar* was on its way into port for repairs, the First Lieutenant was well able to look after her in his absence. Leave was promptly granted. The "near relative" was his wife's mother, Mrs. Elizabeth Weyermann. She was buried at St. Andrew Parish Church at Presteigne, Wales.

Upon his return to duty, Baker received orders from Vice Admiral Saumarez to lead a squadron of four frigates, then being readied in England, to proceed to the Kattegat for the purpose of reinforcing British naval strength in that important waterway. Completion of work on two of the frigates was delayed, and Baker, sensing the time-critical nature of his orders, chose to depart with only the *Tartar* and the *Sheldrake*, Commander James P. Stewart.

The focus of Admiral Saumarez's concern was the Island of Anholt, located midway between Denmark and Sweden, being approximately five miles long and at widest, two miles. Anholt, formerly a part of Denmark, had been captured by British forces in 1809, and now played a strategic role in Baltic Sea naval operations. The island had been fortified, but now in 1811, was protected only by a garrison of some 350 marines with 31 pieces of artillery, under the command of Captain James Wilkes Maurice, designated Governor.[2]

Since 1809, Denmark had nursed the hope of recapturing Anholt, but had been frustrated by the presence of superior British forces in the summer, and ice or stormy weather in the winter. But now, Captain Maurice had reported to Admiral Saumarez, the appearance of an attack force being assembled in the vicinity of Gerrild, a Danish harbor approximately 30 miles southwest of Anholt. That information was correct, but the size of the Danish force was even larger than suspected. It consisted of over 800 marines to be carried by twelve transports, protected by over 200 seamen in twelve gunboats, each mounting six guns.

The Danish flotilla got underway on March 26, 1811, the same day that Captain Baker arrived with the two 32 gun frigates. They anchored on the north side of the island, near a small schooner stationed at Anholt, and out of sight of the Dane's planned approach from the southwest. The next morning, Danish troops under the cover of a thick fog, landed on the west and south sides of Anholt. Governor Maurice had taken the precaution of stationing picket guards all around the island and thus received a prompt alert as to what was happening.

He personally organized and lead his marines to resist the attack. Meantime, Captain Baker directed the *Sheldrake* and the small schooner to remain in place, and provide supporting gunfire while he deftly maneuvered *Tartar* around the east point of the island to attack the Danes on the south side. Cannon fire from Maurice's

Captain.
Leo Cooper, Publisher, London.

shore batteries, plus gunfire from *Sheldrake* and the schooner, blunted the initial attack, killing the Danish commander and his third officer. And when the *Tartar* loomed out of the fog, bringing the Danes under its 32 guns, the attack collapsed. Some 520 Danes surrendered. The rest fled to the west end of the island, where they reembarked the transports and gunboats. These were pursued by the *Tartar* and the *Sheldrake* resulting in the capture of five boats, a few hundred more troops, and a substantial amount of provisions.

Based on the recommendation of Governor Maurice, Captain Baker received a special commendation from Vice Admiral Saumarez—a fine start for a new year, but the year was yet young!

There was little or no time for victory celebrations—the eastern Baltic was plagued with privateers, plundering English trading vessels. To cope with this menace, a secondary Baltic fleet headquarters was established at Hano Bay, at the southeast tip of Sweden, and designated Fort George. It was an assembly point for forming convoys of transports heading through the narrow passage between Sweden and Denmark and thence to England. It was also the operations control center for the frigates attempting to deal with the privateer problem.

Captain Baker and the *Tartar* were assigned to the Hano Bay headquarters, with Baker to lead a two ship squadron, including the *Ethalion*, 36 guns, (152x38). His operating area was the westerly coast of what is now Latvia and Estonia, as far north as the gulf of Finland. Through the summer of 1811 the squadron's operation was very successful, particularly as measured by the taking of nine prize vessels. Of course, after each capture, it would be necessary to transfer a few crewmen from either *Tartar* or *Ethalion* to the prize, to deliver it to Hano Bay. By August the ranks of special "ratings" were somewhat thin, but the time was short till winter weather would curtail operations in any event.

At about noon on August 18, 1811, Baker ordered *Tartar* to put into a bay on the north side of Dago Island. He had designated it as a rendezvous point with the *Ethalion*. Dago Island lies off the west coast of Estonia, of which it is part, and where it is now known as Hiiumaa Island. Dago Island, then technically part of Russia, was in friendly hands, populated by descendants of Teutonic Knights, who were quite willing to sell visiting ships such as *Tartar*, a resupply of fresh meat and produce. As *Tartar* approached an anchorage in an area they had previously visited, Baker heard one of the worst sounds a seafaring man can experience, the ugly thump of his ship striking bottom. At first dismissed as an event of little consequence, it soon became apparent that serious damage had been done—water was pouring into the ship in quantities that could not be stemmed.

There ensued an around-the-clock heroic effort to save the ship, but after three days there was no alternative but to beach her on a sand island in the bay. *Ethalion* remained out of sight, having anchored on the far side of the north tip of the island, but there is little more her crew could have done in any event. Baker sighted and signalled in a small brig, *HMS Woodlark*, and on August 23, dispatched her to Hano Bay with a letter report. No one who has not had the experience of accidently grounding a vessel, even a small one, can possibly sense the mortification Captain Baker felt as he wrote that letter.

HMS Tartar—Aground in Worms Road
23rd August 1811

Sirs,
I feel very deep concern in acquainting you that His Majesty's Ship under my command is lying on shore in Worm's Road, bilged and full of water, and I fear there is not hope to be entertained of saving her from total wreck. To account for this misfortune, I must inform you that on the 18th Inst. (August) about noon, while working into a bay on the Island of Dago, formed by the two points of Dagerort and Simperness, (to which anchorage we had been accustomed to repair for supplies of fresh beef and vegatables) the latter point bearing ENE from compass, dist. about 3.5 miles, the ship on the starboard tack with the wind about WNW, we suddenly shoaled our water from 9 to 6 fathoms, and the next cast of the lead to five fathoms, when (the hands having been 10 minutes previously turned up to tack) the helm

was put alee and the ship came round, but in doing so, shoald her water to 3.5 & 3 fathoms, and after the head yards were braced round and full, she struck lightly forwward, and came up again into the wind. She was directly boxed off but got a little stern way, during which she struck again twice, first under the mizen chains, and lastly about the stern post, when she gained her headway again, and was immediately in 5 fathoms water. The whole transaction I am certain did not last a minute, and she struck so light that neither myself or any other person had the least idea of her having received the slightest damage. The wind was moderate and the water smooth—however on sounding the well about five minutes after the accident had happened, the ship was found to have nearly a foot water. The chain pumps were immediately put to work and the leak gaining, I ran into these Roads, and anchored the ship in the hope of stopping or at least rendering it more under control. We accordingly got our sails under her bottom with yarns, blankets, etc. and tried every method that suggested itself to my own experience, as also whatever was thought of by others in the ship but without making any impression whatever at any one time on the leak, which by clearing the bread and spirit rooms, and cutting away the ceiling, water found to arise from the space between the sternpost and step of the mizen mast, where the water continued to rush in with great and uninterupted violence. One of the men also who dived under the ship's bottom said that he felt the garboard strake rent from the keel in that part so wide that he could put his hand into it. Notwithstanding these discouraging circumstances the men continued to work at the pumps with uncommon animation as long as human nature could support the fatigue.

On Monday the guns were thrown overboard with a hope that by lightening the ship the water would not pour in so fast but this measure had no effect whatever, and on Wednesday, having been there three days and three nights with the pumps never stopping for a single moment but to change the —— the people were become quite exhausted and wholly incapable of any further exertions the leak consequently gained rapidly, and I had no prospect of ever saving the lives of the crew but by running the ship on shore, which I accordingly did about noon of that day, near a sandy island on the western side of the roadstead. She filled in about 3 hours after the pumps had ceased; as I had been unfortunately without the assistance of the HMS Ethalion all the time, who had stood out of sight to the northward, in the morning

Frigate, similar to Baker's, H.M.S. Tartar.

of Sunday, before our disaster happened. I proceeded to erect tents on the little island, to hold the people, and began to get out the provisions and stores, in which we are still employed. Yesterday the HMS Woodlark appeared in sight, and I called her in and shortly afterward the Ethalion was seen and also called, but unhappily, in coming in she went on shore on the middle ground, and lay for six hours, when she was again got off; and I understood by a telegraphic (signal flags) message that she sustained but little injury; however as I hope to save the greater part of the ship's furniture and stores, and as the Ethalion will not be able to contain the whole together with the people, I have thought it best to dispatch the Woodlark immediately to appraise you of our situation. In the meantime I shall continue to clear the ship, and have everything ready to put on board any transport or other vessel you may think proper to send; and after she is cleared, unless I should see any disposition on the part of the enemy to disturb us, I shall let her remain where she is until I have your order to destroy her, or otherwise; but while the Ethalion remains by us, I do not expect any hostile visit from the Russians. Indeed the Barons Hernberg of the Island of Dago, have hitherto offer'd and given us all their assistance that I requested.[3]

> *I have the honor to be*
> *Sir*
> *Your very obedient*
> *humble servant*
>
> *Joseph Baker, Captain*

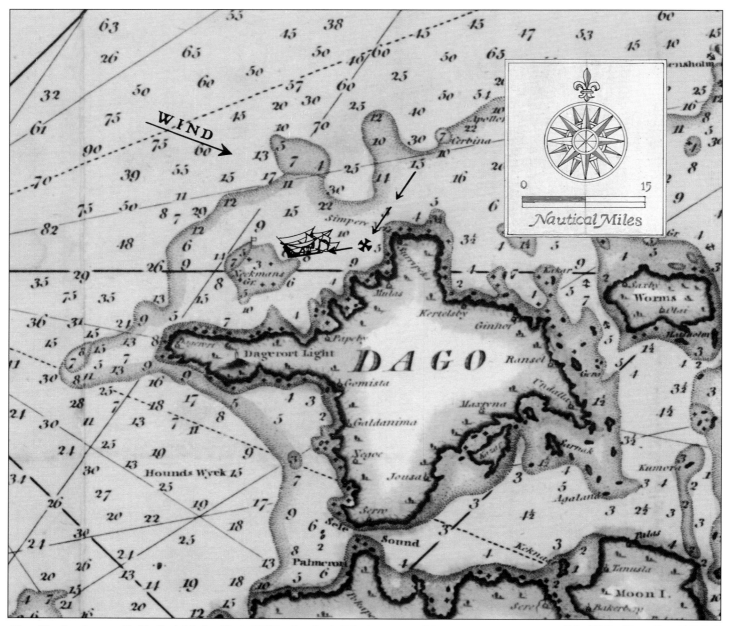

Dago Island as shown on the Heather's Marine Chart of 1808, referred to in Baker's court-martial proceedings.
Notations have been added to indicate the path of H.M.S. Tartar before and after striking bottom.

National Maritime Museum, Greenwich, England.

Rocky shoreline near location where
H.M.S. **Tartar** *was wrecked.*

Meri Mu Meri, Estonia.

Leadsman casting his line to measure water depth.
Leo Cooper, Publisher, London.

At Hano Bay the reaction was entirely predictable—news of the loss of the *Tartar* was "bucked up the line" to Vice Admiral Saumarez at Winga Sound, and thence to the Admiralty in London, and Captain Wilkinson with the *Courageux* was immediately sent to Dago Island to lend what assistance he could. Considerable amounts of hardware and supplies were salvaged. Captain Wilkinson concurred with Captain Baker's recommendation that the remains of *Tartar* be torched. If his first command ship is the best sight a young naval officer can see, then for a senior captain, the sight of his last command burning on the beach in the Baltic Sea has got to be the worst!

The non-combat loss of a naval ship mandated a court-martial proceeding just as it would today. Vice Admiral Saumarez ordered the proceeding held aboard *HMS Vigo*, 74 guns, in Winga Sound, on October 23, 1811.

The importance attached to the proceeding is indicated by the stature of the review board he appointed; Rear Admiral Manby Dixon, President, Rear Admiral George Johnstone Hope, Vice President, and twelve Captains. And this was not just a collection of arm-chair officers; two had fought with Nelson at Trafalgar, and five others had held command roles in major combat.

After an introductory statement by Captain Baker (similar but not identical to his letter of August 23rd), testimony was taken from each of *Tartar's* officers and several of the crew. Attention was focused on previous visits into the bay at Dago Island, the information shown (and not shown) on charts in current use, and the steps taken in the unsuccessful effort to save the ship. A hand-written record of the entire proceeding was located in the archives at Kew, England, and was transcribed and included in Appendix A. It

Vice Admiral Sir James Saumarez, Commander of England's Baltic fleet in which Joseph Baker served as a senior captain.

James Saumarez

constitutes one of the best accounts that the author has seen, explaining the operation of a circa 1800 sailing ship. Members of the legal profession will welcome this testimony to the productivity of the adversarial process.

The record includes a tragi-comical account of Private Thomas Browne, a hapless young marine, who after being caught filching his sergeant's grog, fell into a sequence of aggravated misbehavior, leading to a sentence of 150 lashes. The almost unheard of severity of that sentence is indicated by the scribbled underline for emphasis on the original document.

The formal findings of the court-martial board are also part of Appendix A. In summary, they found that the available charts gave no indication of the shoal *Tartar* struck, that the "..exertions to save her were highly meritorious," and therefore they acquitted Captain Baker, his officers and crew of all blame for the loss of the *Tartar*.

Before leaving this episode, two aspects are worthy of comment. Experienced sailors, reading the full court-martial transcript, may have difficulty relating the reported striking of a shoal, with the description of the vessel's subsequent behavior. The reported damage to the garboard strake suggests rather a large submerged, isolated rock as the villainous obstruction. A photograph taken in much more recent years, shows just that sort of rock on a nearby beach. If the geologic origins of the area included a number of such specimens, above and below water, then the modified explanation of the "striking" might better fit. And finally, residents of western Washington and British Columbia, particularly those familiar with hull repair techniques used by Vancouver, will wonder why Baker didn't simply beach *Tartar* between tides, make temporary repairs, and head for the nearest friendly shipyard. Furthermore, why did the court-martial board not ask about that alternative? The explanation is that tidal changes in the eastern Baltic Sea are almost negligible. Everyone on the court-martial board knew that, and so the question was never asked.

Baker's next and final active duty station is reported to have been as commanding officer of a French prisoner-of-war camp at Stapleton, Avon, only a short distance from the city of his birth, Bristol. He arrived there early in 1812. The prisoner population consisted mainly of seamen captured in naval blockade engagements over the past decade. They numbered over 2,000, some having been held there for as long as ten years. It must have been dreary duty for sea captain Baker, but it did afford him more frequent opportunities to get home to Presteigne, some 70 miles to the north. In any event, the assignment would not last long. In the spring of 1814, following his disastrous expedition to Russia, Napoleon was forced to abdicate and was banished to the Island of Elba in the Mediterranean Sea. The concurrent Treaty of Paris provided for the return of all prisoners. The camp at Stapleton was closed.

Most everyone thought the long years of war in Europe were over, everyone but Napoleon that is. Droves of navy officers were put on inactive duty, and

French prisoner of war camp near Bristol, England.

Gentleman's Magazine, May 1814.

that included Captain Baker. He returned to Presteigne, and for the first time in the seventeen years of his marriage, he was able to be a full-time father and husband. His fatherly attentions had to be divided among the six children then at home, ages one through eleven. The oldest, James Vashon Baker, age 16, was already following his father's footsteps as a navy midshipman. Two more children were yet to arrive, Elizabeth Catherine in 1815, and Joseph Jr. in 1817. Joseph Baker must have felt fortunate indeed for the home and affection which now focused his attentions and filled his hours. Even his old shipmate, Peter Puget, who still owned a home just a block away, was not available for swapping sea stories. He was still on active duty, but at a desk job out in India.

On February 26, 1815, Napoleon escaped from Elba, and started on the rampage that would finally end four months later at the battle of Waterloo. On April 18, Joseph Baker wrote a letter to the Admiralty, asking for an active duty assignment "..in the command of any ship and on any station their Lordships may do me the honor to appoint." Quite possibly he expected another build up of naval forces to contain Napoleon, and wanted to express his loyalty and readiness to serve. Or was he missing the salt air and the sea legs he couldn't find in

Presteigne? Experienced navy hands would be inclined to label Baker's request as a futile gesture, citing the unwritten rule that a captain who had lost a ship would never get another command. But the fact was that barring a reexpansion of the fleet, there simply were no commands available. Even his friend Captain Puget, who had more seniority on the captains list, and whose combat career had ended in a blaze of glory at the Second Battle of Copenhagen, had had to find satisfaction in an administrative assignment as Naval Commissioner at Madras. Certainly Baker didn't believe he was making a futile gesture, but no record has been found of any response to his request.

Joseph Baker's request for sea duty certainly indicates that he was in good health and feeling strong in mid-year 1815. And even well into 1816, he was not suffering any incapacitating malady, judging from the fact that he and Elizabeth were continuing to add to their family. But 1817 brought a rather sudden change in Joseph's health, the exact nature of which is not revealed by any available record. Newspapers of the day carry no reports of any epidemic disease, nor is there any record of concurrent serious illness among other members of the family. However, in the Town of Hereford, some twenty miles southeast of Presteigne, the Journal of July

St. Andrew Parish Church, Presteigne, Wales,
where Captain Joseph Baker was buried.

2, 1817 carried the sad news that, "On Thursday last died at Presteigne, universally esteemed and lamented Captain Joseph Baker, R.N.".

Judged even by the shorter life spans of the day, Joseph Baker's life would have to be described as brief, but full. He had seen more of the world than most, then and now. Professionally, his skills in cartography produced the first comprehensive charts of the west coast of North America, charts which would be used by mariners and appreciated by historians for generations. He would be denied the pleasure of sharing with his beloved wife Elizabeth, the joys of seeing their children mature, inspired as they were by his example of devotion to service.

Joseph Baker was buried in the cemetery of St. Andrew Parish Church of Presteigne, Wales. Carved in a memorial stone mounted in the sanctuary are the words;

Sacred to The Memory of
Joseph Baker Esq.
Post Captain in the Royal Navy
who died June 26th 1817 age 49.

As one lingers in this peaceful village churchyard on a warm spring day, the most appropriate thoughts would seem to be those expressed by Robert Louis Stevenson;

Home is the sailor, home from the sea,
And the hunter home from the hill.

CHAPTER 9

Epilogue

The group gathered for Joseph Baker's funeral included a number of close friends and family prepared to console and assist Elizabeth as she faced a difficult future. Her aunt, Mrs. Hollitt, lived close by, but was now 84 years old. One of her closest friends, Hannah Puget, lived just a block away, having recently returned from India. Captain Peter Puget was enroute home from India, soon to be retired. But as had been the case throughout her life, the most "solid rock" upon whom she could lean in time of need, beyond Joseph, was "Uncle Jim" Vashon. It was to him that Elizabeth's children would now look for fatherly guidance. That surely gave him plenty to ponder as he and his wife, Sarah, rode their carriage the fifteen miles of country road back to their home in Ludlow.

The oldest son, James Vashon Baker, was already away pursuing a naval career, which would ultimately carry him to the rank of Admiral. The younger children presented a wide range of demands, from the second son, Casper Weyerman Baker, 14, already showing an aptitude for advanced education, to the tenth and youngest child, Joseph, only recently born.

Elizabeth's dear friends, the Pugets, moved to Bath, some 70 miles to the south in 1818. The ailments Captain Puget had accumulated in India seemed to be eased by his taking an occasional "course of the waters" at the renowned Bath hot springs. In June of 1820, Elizabeth's aunt, Mrs. Hollitt, died at age 87, and was laid to rest in St. Andrew Parish Church cemetery. With nothing remaining to hold her in Presteigne, Elizabeth moved her family to Ludlow to be closer to Uncle Jim Vashon and Aunt Sarah.

The next five years was a period of serenity and relative security for Elizabeth. Her children seemed to be making the kind of progress every parent could hope for. Casper had been admitted to Oxford University. The younger boys were enrolled in the highly regarded Ludlow Grammar School, already established for over 500 years, and still very much in business in 1992. The fourth son, William Erskine Baker, was showing outstanding abilities in mathematics, and an interest in a military career. No one could have imagined the agonies that lay in Elizabeth's path.

In 1826, Casper died, shortly after receiving his B.A. degree from Oxford. Just one year later, the third son, Peter Puget Baker, after launching a career in commerce as a clerk at the Bank of England, died. Later that same year, Uncle Jim, Admiral James Vashon Baker, died October 20, 1827, at the very advanced age of 85. The agony rolled on.

In the spring of 1828, William Erskine, now a lieutenant in the Royal Engineers, prepared to depart for an assignment in India. He had been one of Elizabeth's favorites, a frail youth who had required much of her devotion to build his strength and overcome a speech defect. She was very proud of the accolades he had won in mathematics at Addiscombe, and of his appointment as an officer, and the thought of his departure was devastating. In a plethora of grief, Elizabeth penned "dear Willie" a farewell letter with such beauty and emotion that he carried it in his most treasured papers for the rest of his life. (The main body of the letter is reproduced below.) It gives copious testimony to the character, the intelligence, and the strength of this woman with whom Joseph Baker had been fortunate enough to share his life.

I thought, my dear Will, that I could say so much to you before we parted, but I feel I cannot. I am so much confused by grief that when I see you I forget it all; now that I am writing, my thoughts and feelings are so mingled together, I know that when my letter and you are gone I shall remember many things I meant to say and did not.

I should have thought myself very neglectful had I not done everything in my power to provide for your bodily comforts: surely the mother acts rightly who proves that, to her, the soul of that child is most valuable.

Don't be afraid, my dear Willie, that I am going to give you a great deal of advice after this long preamble. I am only going to tell you what I think, and what I can think about; for, in speaking of religion, I am very fearful to injure the Devine cause I am pleading for. Snow must be touched only by delicate clean fingers, if we would preserve its whiteness unsullied; it is the same way with religion. But I must speak, and may God, who sees my intentions, give his blessing to them.

You are going, my beloved son, into countries where the name of our Saviour is unknown or disregarded—where perhaps the only temple for his worship may be your own heart; guard then, the issues of that heart. Watch and pray that it may become pure and holy; and never forget God in a strange land. Be like Abdiel in Milton, whose simple faithful character we must admire—

> *"His loyalty to Right, his love, his zeal;*
> *Not number, nor example with him wrought,*
> *To swerve from truth, or change his constant mind,*
> *Tho' single'—*

Oh, my son, my own dear son! let Religion possess the first place in your every thought and action: it will not consent to hold a second place; it must be no theory, but practice. It must be mingled with all your thoughts. Do not suppose I would wish to appear superior, or pretend to eloquence. I only wish to touch your heart with that pure and glorious truth, with that joyful hope, which now makes me indeed reckon the sufferings of the present time as not worthy to be compared with the glory which shall be revealed to us. Soon, very soon, you will be removed where everything around you (is) different, in another quarter of this immense world; but, with God, this immense world is but a little speck, and god will be with us both at the same time: we may both be kneeling to him at the same hour; and to him we shall appear very near to each other.

Think how I shall be repaid for all my sorrows by your return. Be careful then of your health. And should we never meet again on this earth, accept, my dear Will, of my sincere and heartfelt thanks for your affectionate conduct and industry. To say I love you and pray for you would be only repeating what I am sure you are convinced of; but till you are a parent, and the only parent, you can never know the painful solicitude of my heart. To the protection and care of Heaven I commend you, my beloved son. Adieu,—Elizabeth Baker.

William spent nearly thirty years out in India, winning great commendations for his work in developing flood control and irrigation systems, and later railroads. He rose to the rank of General, and received the honor of Knight Commander of the Bath.[1] But Elizabeth's premonition proved correct—she never saw him again, for it was not until 1848 that he was given leave to visit England. One of his fellow officers, Colonel John Colvin, did return to England in 1838, and married William's older sister, Joseph and Elizabeth's fourth child, Josephine Puget Baker. But before that happy occasion, Elizabeth had to endure one more tragic event. In 1836, her sixth son, Henry Whittaker Baker, died at age 23, just after passing the examinations for entry into the medical profession. Possibly present to console her at that sorry time, were the oldest son, James, the fifth son, Vashon, who had also chosen a career in the navy, and of course, Josephine plus the youngest daughter, Elizabeth, and the youngest son, Joseph, who was preparing for a career as a clergyman.

Elizabeth died in 1841, and was buried at St. Laurence's Parish Church in Ludlow. Carved in her memorial stone are the words:

> Sacred to the Memory of
> Elizabeth Baker, widow of
> Capt. Joseph Baker, R.N.
> and niece of Admiral Vashon
> she died Feb. 14, 1841, age 65 y.
>
> Blessed are the dead which
> die in the Lord and so
> sayeth the spirit, for they
> rest from their labors and
> their works do follow.

Of the six of Baker's children who lived to maturity, three were particularly fruitful, James Vashon Baker, Josephine Puget Baker Colvin, and Vashon Baker. Their presently living descendants are of the fourth, fifth, and sixth generations, and a full display of the family tree would require a wall-size chart. A study of the record reveals something of the standards of achievement which Joseph held, and passed on to his children. Of his seven sons and son-in-law, there emerged one Admiral, one General, one Navy Captain, and one Army Colonel. From ten grandsons, there were added one Admiral, two Army Colonels, and one Navy

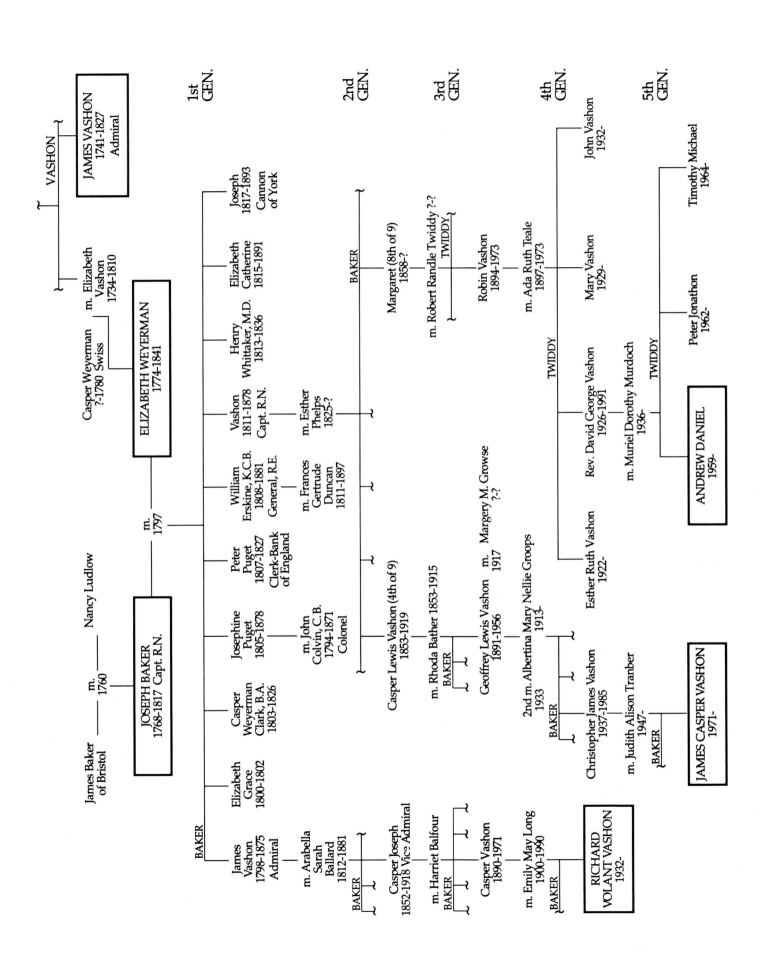

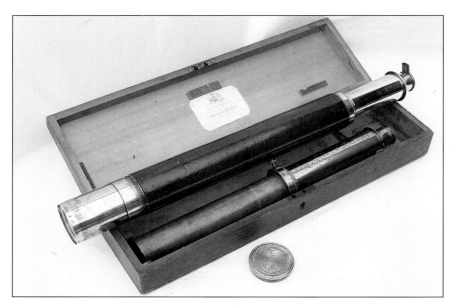

Baker's telescope.

Lieutenant. Service to King and country was held in high esteem. Service to God and church was apparently also well regarded, judging from the significant number of clergymen shown on the family tree. The pursuit of wealth must not have enjoyed equal esteem. One of Joseph's grandsons who emigrated to Argentina, and became a railroad magnate, is labeled on one family tree as the "black sheep."

Present day members of the family have also demonstrated a genuine interest in preserving family history, a fact which has repeatedly been of great assistance to the author. Richard Baker, of Inverness, Scotland, a descendant of Joseph's oldest son, provided the photocopies of Joseph and Elizabeth Baker's portraits, together with extensive family tree diagrams. James Casper Vashon Baker, of Leicester, England, a descendant of Joseph's fifth son, Captain Vashon Baker, furnished a photo of Joseph's inscribed telescope, plus additional family tree data. The Twiddy family, also descendants of Captain Vashon Baker, including Ruth

Vashon Twiddy Woolley, Rev. David Vashon Twiddy, Mary Vashon Twiddy Blount, John Vashon Twiddy, all of Ludlow, England, plus Andrew Daniel Twiddy of Nanaimo, British Columbia, have been especially helpful. They provided a wealth of information on family history, and introduced the author to the charms of Ludlow, the Welsh village of Presteigne and the beautiful countryside of The Midlands.

Just as a well designed musical composition ends on a note of the original theme, the conclusion of the Joseph Baker story takes us back to the beginning—to Mt. Baker. Andrew Daniel Twiddy, associated with Malaspina College, lives in the Vancouver Island City of Nanaimo, within sight across the Georgia Straits of beautiful Mt. Baker. His oldest son, James Joseph Baker Twiddy, great, great, great, great grandson of Captain Joseph Baker, can now observe the mountain, visit the mountain, and is learning to share in the timeless wonderment that Joseph experienced when first he beheld it on a pleasant April afternoon just 200 years ago.

St. Laurence's Parish Church, Ludlow.

The following account of Captain Joseph Baker's court-martial is a transcription of the hand-written record on file at the Public Record Office at Kew, England. Grammar, spelling and punctuation have been retained with a few additions for clarity. Where a blank is indicated, a word was simply unreadable. Marginal clarity is indicated by (?).

A Court Martial assembled and held on board HMS Vigo in Winga Sound, Gothenburg (Sweden) the 23rd of October 1811.
Present
Manby Dixon, Esq., Rear Admiral of the Red and second officer in command of His Majesty's Ships and Vessels in Winga Sound, Gothenburg,—President.
George Johnstone Hope, Esq., Rear Admiral of the Blue, First Captain of HMS Victory.
Captains
Samuel Hood Linzee
Thomas Eyles
Robert Honyman
John Quilliam
Philip Pipon
Philip Wilkinson
Sir Arch. Coll. Dickson
John Serrell
Philip Dumaresq
Manley Hall Dixon
The Court (being duly sworn agreeably to act of Parliament) in pursuance of an order from Vice Admiral Sir James Saumarez, Commander in Chief, dated the 22nd October 1811 and directed to the President, proceeded to try Captain Joseph Baker, the officers and ships company of His Majesty's late ship Tartar for the loss of that ship, by her having struck in a bay in the Island of Dago on the 18th day of August last; and having made all possible enquiry into the circumstances attending the loss of said ship, the Court finds that it happened in consequence of her striking upon a shoal in a bay in the Island of Dago between Simperness and Dagerort on the 18th of August last, which is not laid down in any chart, and are of opinion that no blame whatever is imputable to Captain Baker, his officers and ships company for the loss of the said ship; but on the contrary that their conduct and exertions in trying to save her was highly meritorious, they do therefore hereby fully acquit Captain Baker, his officers and ship's company of all blame for the loss of the said ship, and they are hereby fully acquitted with the exception of Thomas Browne, Private Marines who appears by the evidence produced before the court to have been punished by Captain Baker for improper conduct towards his officer on the 23rd of August last and to have behaved in a blasphemous and insolent manner (after receiving the said punishment) to Captain Baker and the other officers then present, for which latter offence they do adjudge him to be (stripped?) of all the pay and wages due to him and to receive one hundred and fifty lashes on his bare back with a Cat of Nine Tails on board of such ship and at such time as the Commander in Chief shall think proper to direct, and he, the said Thomas Browne is hereby so sentenced accordingly.
Signed by the Deputy Judge Advocate

The transcription of the detailed proceedings follows:

Thence
The prisoners were brought into Court by the Provost Marshal and audience admitted.
Court: Captain Baker have you any charge to prefer against the officers of His Majesty's late ship Tartar?
Answer: No—not any.
Court: Have you any charge to prefer against any of the Warrant and Petty Officers and crew of the Tartar?
Answer: None, with the exception of the man mentioned in my narrative of the loss of the Tartar.
The Court then asked the officers and crew of the Tartar if they had any charges to prefer against their Captain. When they answered "No, none whatever."
The letter from Captain Baker enclosing the statement of the loss of His Majesty's late ship Tartar was read as follows:
His Majesty's Ship Courageux

Winga Sound, 22nd October 1811
I have the honor to enclose for your information a statement of the circumstances which occassioned the loss of His Majesty's Ship Tartar late under my command.
I am, Sir
Your Very obedient humble servant
Joseph Baker, Captain

To:
Sir James Saumarez
Vice Admiral of the Red
On the 18th of August, about noon while turning His Majesty's Ship under my command into a bay in the Island of Dago formed by the two points of Dagerort and Simperness (the anchorage at which we obtained our supplies of fresh beef and vegetables) and also the rendezvous I had appointed for His Majesty's Ship Ethalion to join me about this period, Simperness Point bearing ENE 1/4 E per compass, distance about 3-1/2 miles with Kekki (?) Church S 1/2 W, the ship on the starboard tack with the wind from WNW to NW and the general soundings from 9 to 10 fathoms, which on laying off the bearings appeared to agree with the soundings in the chart. We came suddenly upon 6 fathoms, and the next cast of the lead taken as quick as could be into 5 fathoms when the helm was instantly put alee and the ship came round, but in so doing she shoaled the water to 3 fathoms and after the head yards were braced round and all full on the larboard tack, she struck the ground lightly forward and came up again up into the wind: she was directly boxed off but got a little sternway during which she struck twice, first under the mizen chain, and lastly about her heel when she gained head way and was immediately in 5 fathoms. The whole transaction occupied less than a minute of time and the ship struck so light that neither the man who was at mast head on the foremast or the purser who was sitting below in his cabin were aware that she had touched the ground. I had not myself the most distant suspicion that the ship had sustained any material injury the wind being moderate and the water smooth: my surprize was therefore very great when on sounding the well she was found to be making at the rate of a foot of water in 5 minutes. The chain pumps were immediately got to work but the leak gaining, I determined on running into Worms Road and anchoring there in the hopes of contriving some means of stopping or at least rendering it more under control. About 3 o'clock in the afternoon we anchored and having ascertained by clearing the bread and spirit rooms, and cutting away the ceiling in those parts, that the leak was somewhere abaft between the stern post and step of the mizen mast from whence the water continued to rush into the spirit rooom with great and uninterrupted violence. The spritsail which had been thickly thrummed with shakings etc. was got under the ship's bottom in that part and kept as close as possible to it by proper strappings but without in the slightest degree diminishing the influx of the water. It being supposed from the report of one of the men who dived under the ship's bottom that the injury was in the garboard strake on the starboard side, I caused a spar to be very thickly covered with long shakings well seized one which were got over and to all appearances very accurately placed and secured along the keel where the injury was supposed to be, but this also failed of having any effect.
I continued to use every idea that suggested itself to my own experience as well as whatever was thought of by others in the ship until her bottom was completely wrapped in canvas, and great quantities of oakum, blanket stuff etc. was sunk within it in the hope that some of these substances might be drawn into the leak. On Tuesday the guns were thrown overboard in the expectation that the ship being relieved from their pressures, the water would not pour in with so much violence, but our hopes and expectations were uniformly disappointed. Notwithstanding these discouraging circumstances, the men continued to work at the pumps with undiminished zeal and animation as long as human nature could support fatigue so severe and incessant, but on Wednesday the 21st having been then three days and three nights with the pumps never

stopping for a single moment but to change(?) their spells: their strength became quite exhausted and wholly incapable of any further exertions. The leak consequently gained and I saw no prospect of saving the ship's stores nor even the lives of the crew but by laying her aground I accordingly fixed upon a small sandy islet (called Neckmans on the chart) on the west side of the roadstead so being the most remote spot from the main land and nearly equi-distant from the Island of Dago and Worms; and about (   ) on that day I directed the cable to be cut and run the ship aground as near to the above mentioned islet as she could be got. She filled in about 3 hours afterwards. The people were immediately employed in erecting tents for their accomodation and in getting the stores, furniture and provisions out of her, the greater part of which we were enabled to save. On the following day the HMS Woodlark appearing in the offing, I called her in by signal and dispatched her with the intelligence of our disaster to Rear Admiral Reynolds at Hano. We were also on the same day rejoined by the Ethalion who remained by us. On the 4th of September the Courageux arrived to our assistance; and on the 6th the people were removed on board of her, but a series of blowing weather intervened until the 20th of the same month when His Majesty's Ship under my command was found to have sunk so deep in the sand as to render any chance of saving her entirely hopeless. She was therefore on the evening of that day with the concurrence and approval of Captain Wilkinson set fire to and abandoned.

Having now detailed the circumstances which led to this unfortunate result, it remains my duty to bear the fullest testimony to the zealous ardour displayed by every officer and man under my command in the exertions they made to save the ship. They worked with one heart and one will justifying by their conduct in this emergency that good opinion which upwards of three years service with them as their Captain has taught me to form, and I do not hesitate to affirm, that if a possibility had existed under the circumstances in which she was placed, to have saved her, their efforts would have prevailed.

Their orderly and respectful conduct while on the island, also merits my approbation with the exception of one man (Thomas Browne, Private Marine) who on the first day he landed, behaved in an insolent and mutinous manner to his officer Lieutenant Butler, R.M. for which he was immediately seized up and punished with 36 lashes, but after he was cast off he continued the disrespectful and mutinous behaviours, cursing and blaspheming and (   ) into the sea for which conduct I sent him on board the Ethalion as a prisoner and he has continued in that ship and the Courageux a prisoner at (   ) until the present time.
(Signed) Joseph Baker, Captain of H.M.S. late Ship Tartar

The officers and crew of the Tartar were then ordered to withdraw except Mr. Andrew Mott, the 1st Lieutenant who was sworn.
Court: You have heard the narrative of Captain Baker read; Do you consider that narrative in every part of it, to be perfectly correct in its statement of the loss of the ship?
Answer: I do in every respect.
Court: Do you know of any means that could have been taken by Captain Baker at the time so as to have prevented the accident that happened?
Answer: I do not know of any that could.
Court: Do you know of any recommendation been given to Captain Baker when turning(?) in to alter the course(?) either by the Pilot or others?
Answer: Not by anybody to my knowledge.
Court: Were all hands upon deck at the time, or only the watch?
Answer: All hands.
Court: What Pilots were on deck?
Answer: I believe both.
Court: Was the Master on board?
Answer: No.
Court: Had either of the Pilots' charge of the ship in particular or were either of them the leading Pilot?
Answer: I did not consider either of them as leading

104

Pilot as they had charge of the ship in their watches.

Court: Had you ever been in this bay between Simperness and Dagerort before in the Tartar?

Answer: Yes twice before.

Court: Did you after the ship struck set the course by compass yourself so as to swear to the bearings marked in the log?

Answer: I did not.

Court: Who had charge of the log book in the Master's absence?

Answer: Mr. Morrison the Master's Mate.

Court: Were any of your boats ahead sounding as you were going into the bay?

Answer: Not any of them.

Court: Where was the Master?

Answer: Away in a prize.

Court: Had the ship been tacked before she was put in stays and grounded?

Answer: Yes she had.

Court: Who worked the ship?

Answer: Myself.

Court: Do you recollect who ordered you to put the ship about, whether the Captain or the Pilots?

Answer: Captain Baker.

Court: What time of day was that?

Answer: I think about nine in the forenoon.

Court: Do you know from your own knowledge whether either or both of the Pilots had told your Captain that they were qualified to take the ship into that anchorage?

Answer: I do not.

Court: Do you recollect what water you carried into the bay the two tacks before you grounded?

Answer: No I do not.

Court: Was the shoal on which you grounded to be seen from the ripple of the water or from any other circumstance?

Answer: No it was not.

Capt. Baker: Do you consider the spot on which the ship grounded as being situated on the east side of the bay where we had anchored three times before?

Answer: I consider it being on the edge of the bay but

not in it.

Court: Do you know if either the Master or Pilots had sounded in that bay when you were there before?

Answer: Yes they had.

Court: What did you consider to be the spaces of that bay, was it a good wide bay for turning in?

Answer: I consider it to be a spacious bay, but from the nature of the shoals on the outside of it as difficult to turn in.

Mr. Mott withdrew and Mr. James George Chubb, 2nd Lieutenant of the Tartar was called in and sworn.

Court: Where were you stationed of the morning when the Tartar grounded in working into the bay?

Answer: On the main deck where I was the whole time.

Court: Do you know anything relative to the cause of the ship's first grounding?

Answer: I was on the main deck and heard the (   ) in the chains call the soundings from 9 to 10 fathoms until about twenty minutes before twelve o'clock. She went from 6 to 5 fathoms and at the same instant the helm was put alee when she struck. She came up in the wind, when the yards were braced abox and she immediately went off. She struck lightly abrest the (   ) and twice afterwards and went off again. This was in the space of a minute. The carpenter sounded the well and finding she did not make any water, went down to see if her rudder was damaged. The gun room ports were in: he felt the tiller and came up again immediately and sounded the well when he found she had made ten inches from the time of his going to the gun room to his coming up again.

Court: You have said that immediately the ship shoaled her water, the helm was put alee: how do you know it?

Answer: I saw it from the main deck.

Court: Do you know to whom the charge was given to turn the Tartar into the bay?

Answer: I do not know.

Court: You have heard the narrative read: do you consider that narrative given by Captain Baker as perfectly correct in its statement of the loss of the Tartar?

Answer: I do.

Court: Were you ever sounding the bay yourself?

Answer: I was not.

Court: Had you ever charge of the ship in working into that bay?

Answer: No.

Capt. Baker: How often had we been in that bay at anchor previous to the accident that befel the ship?

Answer: Three times I think.

Capt. Baker: Do you remember that on our anchoring there the second time, I sent the Pilots or one of them to examine and sound from where the ship lay to the nearest shore and round the western side of the bay in the neighborhood of the shoal called the Neckman's Ground?

Answer: Yes I do.

Mr. Chubb withdrew and Mr. Thomas Westerly Kent, 3rd Lieutenant of the Tartar was called in and sworn.

Court: Where was your station on the morning that the Tartar grounded when turning into the bay?

Answer: On the forecastel.

Court: You have heard the narrative read; Do you consider that the narrative given by Captain Baker as perfectly correct in its statement of the loss of the Tartar?

Answer: I do.

Court: Being on the forecastel, of course you were looking out; was there any remark made by you or any other person present, that the ship was standing into danger?

Answer: Not any.

Court: In what way were you apprized of the ships standing into danger?

Answer: The first soundings I heard were irregular, from 11,10,9 ad then 6 and 5 fathoms—The helm was put alee and in coming up into the wind she appeared to me to strike about the chestree lightly in a few seconds afterward.

Court: You have said that she struck immediately she came up in the wind: had you been sounding that bay yourself?

Answer: I had not.

Court: Do you know who had the charge of working the ship into that bay?

Answer: I do not, as I was on the forecastle, and out of the way of hearing the particulars.

Court: How near were you to the nearest shore when you struck?

Answer: About a mile and three-quarters, it was rather on the lee bow; the wind being from SW to South.

Capt. Baker: Had the ship been at anchor in that bay previous to the time of the accident befalling her?

Answer: She had I believe, twice, if not three times.

Mr. Kent withdrew; when the court asked Captain Baker where the Master was at the time the ship grounded, and Captain Baker replied,

"The Master (Mr. White) was away in a prize: we had taken and manned eight prizes which had taken away all the young men capable of having the charge of them, and the Master was sent away in the ninth vessel, as it appeared to me that I could spare him better than any other officer on board, he being wholly unacquainted with those seas and having two pilots on board whom I thought fully capable of having charge of the ship. One of the pilots were always on deck and when all hands were on deck both pilots were up."

The Court asked Captain Baker which of the pilots he considered as having charge of the ship: when he replied: "I consulted them equally"

Mr. William Tong, Pilot of the Tartar was then called in and sworn.

Court: Were you on deck when the Tartar was turning into the bay?

Answer: I was.

Court: do you consider yourself well acquainted with the bay?

Answer: This was the fourth time we had been there, but I was never in it before going in the Tartar.

Court: Have you ever sounded in that bay?

Answer: I sounded on the Neckmans ground two different times.

Court: Did you ever sound on the shoal where the Tartar struck?

Answer: No never.

Court: Had you as pilot, any other marks for turning in, than those the lead gave you?

Answer: I had not any but what the lead gave me.

Court: To what depth of water could you ( ) in on the starboard tack before you put the helm down?
Answer: Into 5 or 6 fathoms by my own soundings on the starboard tack, the wind being from the West to NW, but in standing on the larboard tack, I only required a little offing.
Court: Do you think that your different soundings if there had been any shoals that you would have discovered them?
Answer: According to my soundings I found from 10 to 5 fathoms round the bay and I found nothing less than what I thought a frigate would float in.
Court: How many miles do you consider the round of the bay?
Answer: I should consider about four leagues from Simperness to Dagerorts light house.
Court: Were there any inlets into the bay?
Answer: There appeared bights but I never was in them.
Court: When the Tartar got suddenly into 5 fathoms water who ordered the helm to be put down?
Answer: The Captain immediately.
Court: Did you apprize the Captain before that it was necessary to put the helm down?
Answer: I cannot say I did, as I did not consider the Frigate was standing into any danger.
Court: What sail was the Frigate standing or turning in under?
Answer: Under double or single reef topsails, courses, jib and spanker.
Court: What kind of weather was it?
Answer: Moderate and clear; the wind was variable from west to NW.
Court: You have heard the narrative read. Do you consider that narrative given by Captain Baker as perfectly correct in its statement of the loss of the Tartar?
Answer: Very much so in everything I can say.
Court: What charts had you in your possession of the Gulph of Finland, besides the King's charts?
Answer: A Russian Atlas and Heathers Charts.
Court: What charts did you go by in turning into the bay?
Answer: Heathers Charts.
Court: Did you when the ship struck take the different

bearings of the ( )?
Answer: I did as near as I could by compass.
Court: How did Simperness bear of you?
Answer: ENE 1/4 E by compass; and Dagerort Light House SW by W 1/4 W; Kekki(?) Church S 1/2 W.
Court: What distance were you from the nearest land?
Answer: About 2 or 3 miles, it bearing S 1/2 W or S 3/4 W.
Court: Did you at any time after the ship struck, sound upon that shoal?
Answer: No.
Court: How far was that shoal from the place where you usually anchored in the Tartar?
Answer: It might be about 3 miles bearing East from the anchorage of the ship.
Court: Have you ever seen any chart wherein that shoal on which the Tartar struck is laid down?
Answer: Never.
Court: How far do you suppose that shoal lies from the body of the Neckmans Ground?
Answer: It was about 6 or 7 miles from the Neckmans Ground, bearing from it about NW(?).
Court: Do you mean that all the bearings given by you to the Court are compass bearings?
Answer: They are all by compass.
Court: Who had charge to the Tartar in working into the bay?
Answer: I had.
Court: Had you ever worked her into that bay before?
Answer: Once before.
Court: From having only once worked in before, do you consider yourself qualified without taking the necessary precaution of having boats ahead to sound?
Answer: From having been once in before, and the soundings by the lead, I did not think there was any occasion for that.
Court: When you were in before had you been sent by Captain Baker to sound?
Answer: Yes.
Court: Did you sound any where near the place where the Tartar struck?
Answer: I did not sound there, but all round the bay I have sounded as far as the Neckmans Ground.

Court: Did you never tell Captain Baker that you felt perfectly qualified to pilot the ship he commanded in and out of the bay where she struck?
Answer: No, I never did.
Court: How came you to have charge of her working in?
Answer: By the chart.
Court: Did you sound on or near the shoal on which she struck afterwards?
Answer: No.
Capt. Baker: Do you remember that I observed to you previous to our so suddenly shoaling the water, that altho the ship looked up to windward of the usual anchorage, I would make another tack before I stood in for it?
Answer: Yes I do.
Capt. Baker: At any former time when we were at anchor at that place, was there time or opportunity sufficient to sound the Eastern as well as the Western side of the bay?
Answer: It commonly blew strong when we were there, and there was not opportunity from that circumstance.
Capt. Baker: Do you remember that my reason for not tacking previous to our shoaling the water, was in consequence of the wind altering which made it doubtful whether we should weather Simperness at a sufficient distance on the larboard tack?
Answer: I do; and Captain Baker asked me whether we should weather it; I replied, it was doubtful as the ship came up from SW by S to WSW.
Mr. Tong withdrew and Mr. John Calves, Pilot of the Tartar was called in and sworn.
Court: Had you any charge of the pilotage of the Tartar on the morning that she grounded on the shoal?
Answer: I considered not.
Court: Was you on the Quarter deck at the time she did ground?
Answer: Yes I was.
Court: Did you ever sound in that bay?
Answer: No.
Court: Did you consider yourself as well acquainted with the pilotage into that bay, as the other pilot?
Answer: I considered myself much the same.

Court: Had you anchored in that bay before and how often?
Answer: Three times before.
Court: Do you remember turning into the bay before?
Answer: Yes.
Court: Do you recollect the shoalest water you had at a former turning into the bay before you put the helm down?
Answer: I do not.
Court: What were the general soundings?
Answer: From 12 to 9 fathoms.
Court: Did the other pilot make any remark to you when standing in on the tack when the ship struck, that she was standing closer to the land than usual?
Answer: I do not recollect his making any remarks—
Court: Did you take the bearings of the land when the ship struck?
Answer: Yes; Simperness bore ENE 1/4 E and Kekki Church S1/2W.
Court: What was your distance from the nearest land?
Answer: About two miles and a half and it bore about S 1/2 W.
Court: Did you consider the other pilot qualified to take charge of the ship in working into the bay?
Answer: I did not.
Court: Did you convey to your Captain your doubts as to the abilities of the other pilot?
Answer: No.
Court: I think you have said that you did not consider yourself as having charge of the ship as pilot on the morning she struck; as the hands were up on deck, did you consider that you were to walk about and not assist the Captain in navigating the ship into that harbour?
Answer: No: I always did assist to the best of my power, and gave the best advice I could.
Court: Did you recommend the ship being put in stays before she struck?
Answer: No.
Court: Did you give any advice to the Captain or the other pilot?
Answer: I did not.
Court: Did you conceive the ship standing into any

danger before she suddenly shoaled the water, and did you see that the soundings given by the man at the lead were correct?

Answer: I did not consider the ship as standing into any danger and Mr. Tong was standing on the gun to observe the soundings.

Court: You have acknowledged that you did not know the place that the ship was going into, and likewise that you did not pay attention to the lead before the ship struck; relate what service you performed on that day.

Answer: I took notice of the ship's courses.

Court: Did the Tartar occupy the (same) anchorage each time she went into that bay?

Answer: Nearly.

Court: How did Kekki Church bear when she anchored, and at what distance?

Answer: Kekki Church bore about SSE and distant about 3 miles, or 3 miles and a half.

Court: How far do you suppose the shoal on which you grounded to be from the place where you usually anchored?

Answer: Between two and three miles.

Capt. Baker: You have said that you did not consider yourself or Mr. Tong qualified to take charge of the ship going into the bay; had you been asked or desired by me at the time of going in when the ship struck, to take charge of her, would you have declined it?

Answer: We had never been in the way we were going and I should have declined taking charge of her.

Capt. Baker: Did you at that time or any time previous, express to me any doubt whatever as to the facility of going into the bay?

Answer: Not to my knowledge—

Mr. Calves withdrew and Mr. John Holmes, Carpenter of the Tartar was called in and sworn.

Court: Where were you when the Tartar struck?

Answer: In my cabin.

Court: What did you do in consequence?

Answer: I immediately went out and sounded the well. I found ten inches of water in her, and sounding the second time (the ship then struck lightly) I perceived no alteration in the water. The ship in coming round hung by the heel which threw the wheel from the men's hands who were steering the ship. I was ordered by Mr. Mott the first Lieutenant to go down to the Gun Room and examine the rudder to see if any damage had been done to it. I came on deck and reported to Captain Baker and the first Lieutenant, that as far as I was able to judge the rudder had sustained no damages—Captain Baker desired me to sound the well, and I answered him that I had done it, and could not find the ship had made any water. Before I had time to leave the quarter deck the Carpenters Mate came up and reported that the ship made water fast—Captain Baker then ordered the chain pumps to be rigged which was immediately done.

Court: How soon from the moment the ship struck did you find that the ship made an unusual quantity of water?

Answer: Between four and five minutes from the time she first struck I sounded the well immediately after the Carpenters Mate reported she was making faster, and found twenty inches in her. I did not perceive that she made any water till she hung abaft.

Court: Did the leak continue increasing?

Answer: I found the ship at all times after she hung abaft to make the same quantity of water, which was four inches per minute: at one time I stopped the pumps working one minute which caused an increase of four inches of water. At another time the pumps stood still five minutes to ascertain what quantity of water in that time the ship had made, which I found to be twenty inches and which was the longest time to the best of my knowledge that the pumps stood still.

Court: Did the pumps of the ship at any time keep her free?

Answer: With both chain pumps we have brought her to ten inches.

Court: How soon was that after the ship grounded?

Answer: About twenty minutes.

Court: After the Tartar was off the shoal and was anchored, did the pumps keep her free?

Answer: About an hour after, she was pumped out to ten inches when she sucked.

Court: Had you at that time the thrummed sail under

her bottom?

Answer: We had.

Court: When Captain Baker directed the cable to be cut with the intention to lay the ship on shore, was the leak so much increased as to considerably gain on the pumps?

Answer: We were pumping from the 18th to about ten o'clock on the 21st, night and day and the people were exhausted, laying in and out of the pumps.

Court: State to the court what the defects of the ship were when the cable was cut.

Answer: The principal defect was the leak in the stern (?) of the ship between the mizen mast and the after part of the ship.

Court: As Carpenter of the ship, from your judgement of the defects as to the leak, and from the length of time the whole of the crew had been kept at the pumps: and supposing the Captain had not ordered the cable to be cut for the purpose of running her on shore, how much longer do you think she could have been kept above water?

Answer: From the exhausted state of the crew and the leak still continuing, I should not believe that she would have been kept afloat for twelve hours.

Court: What length of time did it take to run her on shore after the cable was cut?

Answer: About three quarters of an hour.

Court: When the ship was run on shore state what quantity of water was in her and what state she was in.

Answer: There was three feet of water in the well. I sounded her repeatedly after and found some little veriation in the quantity of water which I alleged to its rise more in the body of the ship.

Court: Was she ever pumped out after being on shore?

Answer: She was brought to suck.

Court: In your opinion as Carpenter of the ship was there any prospect of saving the ship after she was run on shore?

Answer: In my opinion not the smallest and it is my opinion that all and everything was done for the preservation of the ship but to no effect.

Court: After her stores and ships company were taken out of her was anything further done to her hull?

Answer: A number of chain plate bolts and dead eyes were drove out by me and the crew and preserved; her mizen mast, foremast and bowsprint was cut away. When all hope were done away of saving the ship she was set fire to.

Court: Was every means that you could possibly devise adopted to stop the leak previous to her being run on shore and without effect?

Answer: There was every means used.

Court: Were all the stores that could possibly be saved got out of the ship previous to her being burnt?

Answer: Everything.

Court: Could you discern from the inside of the ship where the water rushed?

Answer: Yes, abaft the seat to the timbers on the starboard side, chiefly in the run of the ship.

Court: What was your opinion of it?

Answer: I judged that the skeg of the ship was twisted, and that the garboard strake had started out of the rabbitting of the keel.

Court: Did you recommend the ship being pumped out after she was on shore to try whether the (   ) had stopped the leak?

Answer: I did not.

Mr. Holmes withdrew and the following charts;

The Admiralty Chart

Heathers Chart, and a

Russian Atlas being produced in

the Court, and the Pilots having marked the Tartar's situation on each, no shoal appears to be laid down in them where she struck.

Captain Baker was then sworn.

Court: Relate to the Court the charges against the prisoner after the Tartar was abandoned and the people out of her.

Answer: On the 22nd August, the day after the ship was laid on the ground and after the people were landed on the island, Lieutenant Butler of the Royal Marines came to me with a complaint and represented to me, that the prisoner Thomas Browne had treated him with much insolence and disrespect, which having investigated and finding the complaint justly founded I had him seized up and punished with 36 lashes—after he was cast off from that punishment he behaved in a most (   ) and (   ) manner by endeavoring to break loose from the men I desired to take charge of him, cursing and blaspheming and took his hat off and threw it away from him; In consequence of which I caused him to be sent on board the Ethalion as a prisoner.

Court: Were the officers of the ship present at the time that he behaved in that manner after the punishment?

Answer: Lieutenant Butler (R.M.), Lieutenant Chubb, Mr. Morrison, Masters Mate, and I balieve the Master at Arms.

Court: Was he sober?

Answer: He had been drinking more that his allowance but he was not drunk.

Lieutenant Butler of the Royal Marines of the Tartar was called in and sworn.

Court: Relate to the Court what you know of the charges against Thomas Browne the prisoner.

Answer: On the 23rd August, Sergeant Jones brought a Private Marine to me with a complaint of the prisoner having drank his (the Sergeant's) grog; I immediately went with them to the marine's tent to enquire into the particulars of it: the prisoner's manner and answers were very contemptuous. I then advised him to be careful what he was about; he told me I always had been a (   ) upon him, and he did not care a damn about it. I went to Captain Baker and made the complaint who having enquired into it punished the man for it. During the punishment he made use of blasphemous expressions; one in particular I remember to have heard which was "Bugger his soul if he was guilty," after the punishment Captain Baker ordered him to be cast off; his behavior then very very riotous by endeavoring to tear himself from the Quarter Master and the triangle erected for the punishment; Captain Baker then ordered him to be put into confinement. I dismissed the detachment of marines that had been formed to witness the punishment and had just gone to my tent when I heard Captain Baker order the prisoner on board the Ethalion as a prisoner for mutinous behaviour, which I afterward understood was for throwing his hat into the sea and other improper conduct.

Court: Did you hear the prisoner make use of any mutinous expressions after being cast off from the triangle?

Answer: I did not.

Court: Did you see him behave in an insolent or contemptuous manner to Captain Baker, or any other officers after he was punished?

Answer: His manner I conceived was very contemptuous to Captain Baker and the other officers after he was punished.

Prisoner: Have I ever misbehaved myself as to performing my duty?

Answer: I am sorry the prisoner has asked me the question for I cannot give that character of the man I could wish.

Lieutenant Butler withdrew when Mr. Chubb was again called in and sworn.

Court: Were you present when the prisoner was punished on the 23rd August?

Answer: Yes I was.

Court: Relate to the court what was the behaviour of the prisoner to Captain Baker and the other officers after his punishment.

Answer: Immediately after the prisoner was cast off Captain ordered him apart from the rest of the people, he went away in an improper manner, swearing that he had been punished improperly. Captain Baker ordered him to be put in irons, but on finding there were no irons on shore, he ordered him to be lashed to a spar. During the time they were getting a spar to lash him to, he was swinging his arms and his hat about; my back was turned from him a few seconds, and on my returning round I observed his hat by the water side, he had thrown it as far from him as he could. He was then sent on board the Ethalion as a prisoner for mutinous behaviour.

Court: Did you yourself hear the prisoner make use of any mutinous expressions after being cast off from the triangle?

Answer: I think I heard him say "Bugger his bloddy eyes if he had not been punished wrongfully."

Court: Did you see him behave in an insolent or contemptuous manner to Captain Baker or any other officer after being punished?

Answer: I conceived that his behaviour directly he was cast loose was very contemptuous to Captain Baker and the other officers present.

Mr. Chubb withdrew and Mr. Morrison, Masters Mate of the Tartar was called in and sworn.

Court: Was you present when the prisoner made use of the expressions stated in the charge after he was punished?

Answer: Yes.

Court: Relate to the Court the circumstance.

Answer: After being cast off from the triangle, Captain Baker ordered him close to his tent, I was present at the time when the prisoner took off his hat and hove it towards the sea; he damned and buggered his soul and a great deal of languages like that, knocking his hands about. I called to him and Captain Baker heard me. I told Captain Baker the language the prisoner made use of when he ordered him off to the Ethalion. —Mr. Carrington the Master At Arms heard me challenge the prisoner in his demeanour.

Mr. Morrison withdrew and Sergeant Griffith Jones of the Royal Marines was called in and sworn.

Prisoner: Have I ever disobeyed your orders previous to the Tartar being on shore?

Answer: He never did and was always ready for duty but I think him an ignorant man.

The prisoner having nothing further to offer in his defence, the Court was closed and proceeded to deliberate upon and form the sentences when having made all possible enquiry into the circumstances attending the loss of the Tartar, did find that it happened in consequence of her striking upon a shoal in a bay in the Island of Dago between Simperness and Dagerort on the 18th of August last which is not laid down in any chart, and we are of the opinion that no blame whatever is imputable to Captain Baker his officers or ships company for the loss of said ship, but on the contrary that their conduct and exertions in trying to save her was highly meritorious: The Court did therefore acquit Captain Baker his officers and ships company of all blame for the loss of the Tartar; with the exception of Thomas Browne, Private Marine who appeared by the evidence produced before the Court to have been punished by Captain Baker for improper conduct towards his officers on the 23rd of August last and to have behaved in a blasphemous and insolent manner (after receiving the punishment) to Captain Baker and the other officers present for which latter offence the Court did adjudge him to be stripped (?) of all the pay and wages due to him to receive one hundred and fifty lashes on his bare back with a cat of nine tails onboard of such ship and at such time as the Commander in Chief should think proper to direct.

The Court was then opened audience and evidence again admitted and sentence of full acquittal was passed against Captain Baker, the officers and ships company, except Thomas Browne the Private Marine who was sentenced accordingly.

Signed
Deputy
Judge
Advocate

APPENDIX B

The following partial catalog of the folio appended to Vancouver's three volume journal, includes the eight principal charts prepared by Lieutenant Joseph Baker to record the course of the expedition along the west coast of North America and the islands of Hawaii. Some of these charts include inset detailed exhibits of islands, harbors, etc. and these are also listed. The title block of each of the seven charts of the west coast of North America is essentially identical, as follows:

> A CHART
> Shewing Part of The
> COAST OF N.W. AMERICA
> With The Tracks Of
> His Majesty's Sloop
> DISCOVERY and armed tender CHATHAM,
> Commanded by GEORGE VANCOUVER Esq. and prepared
> under his immediate inspection by Lieut. Joseph Baker,
> in which the
> Continental Shore has been finally traced and determined from
> Lat._____ and Long._____ to Lat._____ and Long._____

Folio Plate No.

3	From Lat. 38° 15′ N. and Long. 237° 27′ E. to Lat. 45° 46′ N. and Long. 236° 15′ E. Inset: Bay of Trinidad (California)
5	From Lat. 45° 30′ N. and Long. 236° 12′ E. to Lat. 52° 15′ N. and Long. 232° 40′ E. Insets: Entrance to Columbia River. Gray's Harbour. Port Discovery
7	From Lat. 51° 45′ N. and Long. 232° 08′ E. to Lat. 57° 30′ N. and Long. 226° 44′ E. Inset: Port Stewart
8	From Lat. 30° 00′ N. and Long. 244° 32′ E. to Lat. 38° 30′ N. and Long. 237° 13′ E. Insets: Entrance to Port San Francisco. Port San Diego.
10	From Lat. 59° 30′ N. and Long. 207° 20′ E. to Lat. 58° 52′ N. and Long. 207° 20′ E. Inset: Port Chatham (Cooks Inlet).
11	From Lat. 59° 45′ N. and Long. 219° 30′ E. to Lat. 59° 56′ N. and Long. 212° 08′ E. Inset: Port Chalmers (Prince William's Sound).

12	From Lat. 57° 07′ N. and Long. 227° 00′ E. to Lat. 59° 59′ N. and Long. 219° 00′ E. Insets: Entrance to Cross Sound. Port Conclusion Port Protection.
15	Sandwich Islands (Hawaiian Islands). Insets: Island of Cocos Part of Gallapagos Isles (Albemarle)

A small scale reproduction of Plate No. 5 (covering Puget Sound) is included in Chapter 4. The approximate coverage of seven of the above listed Plates is indicated by the index chart on the following page. Copies of the full scale charts are retained in the collections of several libraries of Washington, Oregon and British Columbia, including:

Washington State Historical Society, Tacoma, Washington
University of Washington Library, Seattle, Washington
Museum of History and Industry, Seattle, Washington

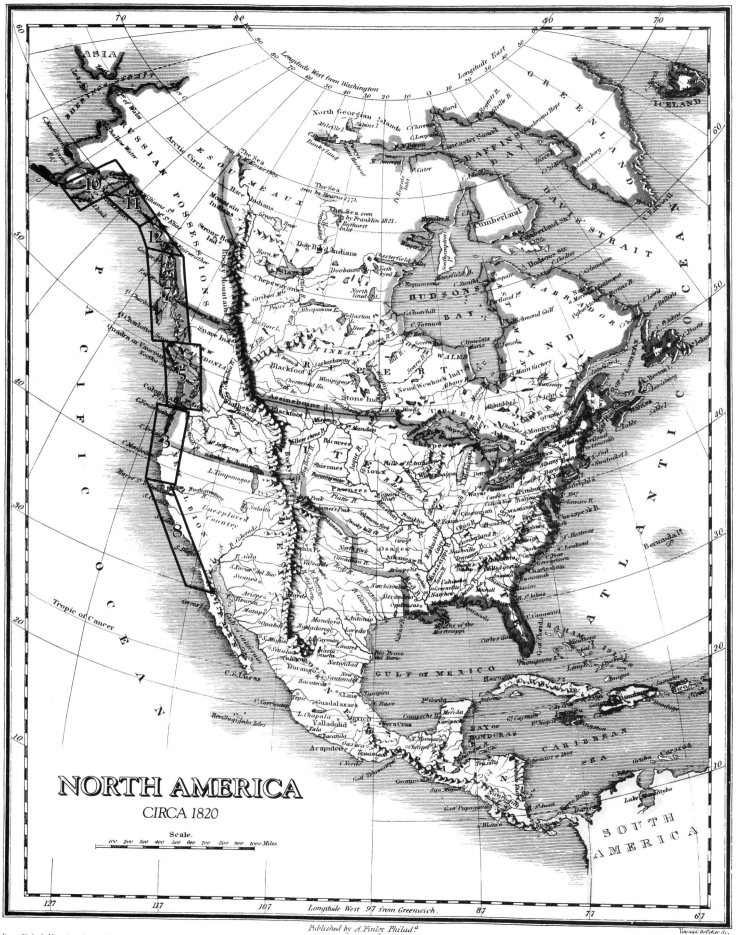

NORTH AMERICA

CIRCA 1820

Scale.

100 200 300 400 500 600 700 800 900 1000 Miles.

Longitude West 97 from Greenwich.

From Finley's New American Atlas

Published by A. Finley Philada.

Young & DeSilver Sc.

Antique Map Number NINE

CHAPTER NOTES

For nautical terminology see Bibliography Reference S-14

Chapter 1
General background—Biblio Ref No's C-1, C-4, C-6, C-8, C-9, S-3, S-6, S-7, S-22.
1. More recent researchers have disputed the precise location of the murders, but there is no dispute as to the identification or location of Destruction Island.
2. At 3 nautical miles per league, equals 51 nautical miles.
3. Biblio Ref S-13.
4. Biblio Ref C-5.
5. Biblio Ref S-12.

Chapter 2
General background—Biblio Ref No's S-1, S-6.
1. Biblio Ref C-7.

Chapter 3
General background—Biblio Ref No's C-1, C-9, S-3, S-11, S-15, S-23.
1. Biblio Ref S-5.
2. The exception was Cranstoun, the ship's surgeon, who remained in a severely debilitated condition. He was sent home aboard the supply ship *Daedalus* in December 1792. Menzies, the botanist, acquired the additional duties of ship's surgeon.

Chapter 4
General background—Biblio Ref No's C-1, C-2, C-4, C-6, C-9, S-3, S-8, S-10, S-15, S-21.
1. A detailed explanation of the methods used in measuring latitude and longitude is included in Biblio Ref C-7. For a simplified description see the appendix of S-24.
2. Vancouver drew heavily on the journals of his subordinates (in this case Baker and Menzies) in drafting his record of the voyage.
3. Literally, May 25, 1660, date of Charles II's return to England: Biblio Ref S-11.
4. Approximately 2 miles south of its presently charted location.
5. Biblio Ref S-8.
6. Biblio Ref S-22.
7. Biblio Ref S-7.

Chapter 5
General background—Biblio Ref No's C-2, C-9, S-3, S-22.
1. Vancouver carried four recently improved models of the spring wound clocks intended to ultimately replace the shore-bound pendulum clocks as a critical part of the equipment for determining longitude. However, the new clocks were not regarded as trustworthy, and in fact, traditional methods of determining longitude were constantly used as a basis for recalibrating the new clocks.

Chapter 6
General background—Biblio Ref No's C-2, C-9, S-3, S-6.
1. After his return to England, Broughton was promoted to Commander and assigned as Captain of the sloop *Providence*. With Mudge as his first Lieutenant and carrying modified instructions for resolving the Nootka question, he sailed from England on February 15, 1795 just as Vancouver was well on his way home. By the time Broughton reached Nootka, March 17, 1796, the Spanish had already abandoned their installations as not worth the upkeep cost. Only a minor Canadian Coast Guard station and the lonely remnants of an Indian village mark the location of this one time center of British and Spanish attention.
2. See Chapter 5, note 1.
3. Bernardo O'Higgins, son of Don Ambrosio, became commander of the Chilean army which in 1818 won freedom from Spain.

Chapter 7
General background—Biblio Ref No's S-1, S-6.
1. Biblio Ref S-9.
2. Biblio Ref S-4.

Chapter 8
General background—Biblio Ref No's C-3, S-1, S-2, S-6, S-18, S-19.
1. Biblio Ref S-24.
2. Biblio Ref No's C-3 and S-1.
3. The phrase "got our sails under her bottom," refers to the procedure call "fothering," placing spare sails under the hull to help stem a serious leak. The "garboard strake" is the name given the two key bottom planks located one on each side of the keel. This letter, written during the turmoil at the time of the wreck, is similar, but not identical, to Capt. Baker's opening statement at the court-martial proceeding, all as included in Appendix A.

Epilogue
1. Biblio Ref S-20.

BIBLIOGRAPHY

Contemporary Sources

C-1 Baker, Joseph (3rd Lieutenant), "A Log of His Majesty's Ship Discovery from 22nd December 1790 to 27 November 1792" (microfilm), University of Washington Library.

C-2 Baker, Joseph (2nd, 1st Lieutenant), "A Log Of His Majesty's Ship Discovery from 28 November 1792 to 1 July 1795," Pro (Public Record Office) ADM 55/33, Kew, London.

C-3 Baker, Joseph (Commander, March 1799,-Captain, April 1802 Correspondence at PRO, Kew, London:
ADM 1/11 CINC Baltic Fleet
ADM 1/13 CINC Baltic Fleet
ADM 1/1549 Captains Letters
ADM 1/1550 Captains Letters
ADM 1/1551 Captains Letters
ADM 1/2165 Captains Letters
ADM 1/4512 Promiscuous Letters
ADM 1/4775 Promiscuous Letters
ADM 1/4836 Promiscuous Letters
ADM 1/5419 Record Office—Courts Martial
ADM 1/1559 Captains Letters—Presteigne, April 1815

C-4 Broughton, William R. Lt. "Log Book Of The Chatham, Tender, Lt. W.R. Broughton, Commander, Sept. 1791-August 1792" (microfilm), University of Washington Library.

C-5 Boit, John "Voyage Of The Columbia Around The World, 1790-1793," Edited by Dorothy O. Johansen, Portland, Oregon, Beaver Books—1960.

C-6 Menzies, Archibald, "Journal Of Vancouver's Voyages, 1792" Edited by C.F. Newcombe, MS, British Museum. British Columbia Archives, Victoria, B.C., 1923.

C-7 Moore, John Hamilton, "The New Practical Navigator," 14th Edition, London, G.G. & J. Robinson—1800.

C-8 Puget, Peter, "A Log Of The Proceedings Of His Majesty's Sloop Discovery, George Vancouver Esq., Commander, Kept By Lieutenant Peter Puget From The 4th Day Of January 1791, To The 14th Day Of January 1793" (microfilm), University of Washington, Seattle.

C-9 Vancouver, George, R.N. "Voyage Of Discovery To The North Pacific Ocean And Around The World," Vol. 1,2,3, Folio. Printed for G.G. & J. Robinson and J. Edwards, London—1798.

Secondary Sources

S-1 Allen, Joseph, R.N. "Battles Of The British Navy," Vols. 1 & 2. London, Henry G. Bohn, 1852.

S-2 Andersen, Henning Soby, "Denmark Between The Wars With Britain, 1801-07," Scandinavian Journal Of History, Vol. 14, No. 3, 1989. The Almqvist & Wiksell Periodical Company, Stockholm, Sweden.

S-3 Anderson, Bern, "The Life And Voyages Of Captain George Vancouver," Seattle, University Of Washington—1960.

S-4 Armet, Helen, "Convoys To The Trade On The East Coast Of Scotland," Edinburgh, The Book Of The Old Edinburgh Club—28th Vol.—1953.

S-5 Beaglehole, J.C., "The Life Of Captain James Cook," Stanford, California, Stanford University Press.

S-6 Colledge, J.J., "Ships Of The Royal Navy," Vol. 1, London, Greenhill Books, Lionel Leventhal Limited, 1987.

S-7 Howay, Frederic W. (Ed.), "Voyages Of The Columbia To The Northwest Coast, 1787-1790 & 1790-1793," Oregon Historical Society Press In Cooperation With The Massachusetts Historical Society, 1990 Reprint, Originally Published in Boston—1941.

S-8 Kendrick, John, "The Voyage Of Sutil And Mexicana 1792," Spokane, Washington, The Arthur H. Clark Co.—1991.

S-9 Lloyd, David J., Ma, MEd, "Country Grammar School," Ludlow, England—1977.

S-10 Mahood, Ian S., "The Land Of Maquinna," West Vancouver, B.C., Agency Press Ltd.—1971.

S-11 Meany, Edmond S., "Vancouver's Discovery Of Puget Sound," Portland, Oregon, Binfords & Mort—1957.

S-12 Miles, John, C., "Koma Kulshan—The Story Of Mt. Baker," Seattle, Washington, The Mountaineers—1984.

S-13 Nokes, J. Richard, "Columbia's River," Tacoma, Washington, Washington State Historical Society—1991.

S-14 "Nautical Terms Under Sail," London, Trewin Copplestone Publishing Ltd.—1978.

S-15 Pethick, Derek, "First Approaches To The Northwest Coast," Seattle And London, University of Washington Press—1979.

S-16 Potter, Norris W. - Kasdon, Lawrence M. - Rayson, Dr. Ann, "The Hawaiian Monarchy," Honolulu, The Bess Press Inc.,—1983.

S-17 Raid, Heiti - Tuulik, Ulo - Jussi, Fred, "Meri Mu Meri," ISBN 5-450-00133-9—1988.

S-18 Scott, Franklin D., "Sweden: The Nation's History," Carbondale, Illinois, Southern Illinois University Press—1988.

S-19 Steiler, Adolf, "Hand - Atlas - 83 Karten," Schweden und Norwegen (No. 17), Gotha: Justus Perthes—1859, University of Washington Library, G1019-S87-1859.

S-20 Yule, H. and Maclagan, R., Cochairmen Of Editorial Committee, "Memoir Of The Career Of General William Erskine Baker, R.E., K.C.B.," London—1882.

S-21 Wagner, Henry R., "Spanish Explorations In The Strait Of Juan De Fuca," New York, AMS Press—1971.

S-22 Walbran, Capt. John T., "British Columbia Coast Names," Vancouver, B.C., J.J. Douglas Ltd.—1971 Edition.

S-23 Whitebrook, Robert Ballard, "Coastal Exploration Of Washington," Palo Alto, California, Pacific Books—1959.

S-24 Wing, Robert C. with Newell, Gordon, "Peter Puget," Seattle, Gray Beard Publishing—1979.

ACKNOWLEDGEMENTS

Many individuals and institutions have assisted the author in assembling and interpreting the large volume of documents, maps, photographs and correspondence necessary to reconstruct the story of Joseph Baker. Others have kindly labored through early drafts of the manuscript and provided helpful critique. The particularly valuable contributions of the following are gratefully acknowledged:

James Casper Vashon Baker (descendant) Leicester, England

Richard Baker (descendant) Inverness, Scotland.

Mary Vashon Twiddy Blount (descendant) Ludlow, England.

Mart Kask, Seattle, Washington, USA— Native of Estonia.

Terje I. Leiren, Ph D., Associate Professor of Scandinavian Studies, University of Washington, Seattle, Washington, USA.

David J. Lloyd, M.A., M.Ed., Ludlow, England.

Keith A. Murray, Ph D., Distinguished Service Professor Emeritus, Western Washington University, Bellingham, WA, USA

David Nicandri, M.A., Director, Washington State Historical Society, Tacoma, Washington, USA.

Major Brian J. Oldham, M.B.E., B.Sc., Harrow, England.

Garry Shalliol, M.A., Washington State Historical Society, Tacoma, Washington, USA.

Andrew D. Twiddy, M.A., (descendant) Nanaimo, B.C., Canada.

Rev. David Vashon Twiddy, B.D., (descendant) Penrith, England.

John Vashon Twiddy, (descendant) Ludlow, England.

Rev. Canon Malcolm Widdecombe, Bristol, England.

James V. Wing, Bainbridge Island, Washington, USA.

Ruth Vashon Twiddy Woolley, (descendant) Ludlow, England.

Georgiana Ballard Wolfe, (descendant) Flintridge, CA, USA.

Archival Institutions

Central Library, George IV Bridge, Edinburgh, Scotland.

National Maritime Museum, Greenwich, England.

Public Record Office (PRO), Kew, London, England.

Washington State Library, Olympia, Washington, USA.

Northwest Collection, University of Washington Library, Seattle, Washington, USA.

Hewitt Library, Washington State Historical Society, Tacoma, Washington, USA.

INDEX